Preaching About Conflict
in the Local Church

Preaching About ... Series

Preaching About Conflict in the Local Church

William H. Willimon

The Westminster Press
Philadelphia

Book design by Gene Harris

First edition

Published by The Westminster Press®
Philadelphia, Pennsylvania

PRINTED IN THE UNITED STATES OF AMERICA

9 8 7 6 5 4 3 2 1

Library of Congress Cataloging-in-Publication Data

Willimon, William H.
  Preaching about conflict in the local church.

  (Preaching about— series)
  Bibliography: p.
  1. Church controversies. 2. Preaching. I. Title.
II. Series.
BV652.9.W54 1987   254   87-8227
ISBN 0-664-24081-X (pbk.)

To my colleagues
at Duke University Chapel

Contents

1

Understanding Conflict

The church board becomes deadlocked over whether or not to endorse denominational support for the National Council of Churches.

The women's Bible study group divides in a debate about biblical interpretation.

The church youth confront the board of deacons concerning the need for more money for youth activities.

At a meeting of the pastoral relations committee, the pastor learns, to her surprise, that her contract is to be terminated at the end of the year because, "You don't visit enough."

Is it possible to bring such congregational problems into the pulpit and use them as sources for sermons? This book is an exploration of the possibilities for preaching to local church problems. It is based on the assumption that sermons are legitimate settings for a pastoral, biblical encounter with intrachurch conflict. The demands of the Christian faith and our attempts to embody that faith in our congregational life are not easy. Conflict is inevitable, and for the preacher to attempt to remove his or her preaching from that conflict is to imply that the Bible is irrelevant for the church today and that preaching is too timid and detached to be of great help when the chips are down and we desperately need a guiding word.

Few of us pastors entered the ministry out of a love of conflict. Even though we know that the Hebrew prophets of old were centers of controversy, even though the Lord himself died amidst struggle and pain, we still hope that there is some way to accomplish significant ministry without risk of conflict. We enjoy thinking of ourselves as reconcilers, peacemakers, and bridge builders. Thus, when conflict occurs and the sparks begin to fly, it is natural for us pastors to ask ourselves, "What did I do wrong to deserve this mess?"

Perhaps these manifestations of deep human feelings, these exposed nerves, are evidence that we are doing our job or that we are at least on our way to doing our job. Often the test of our ministry will be, not the avoidance of all conflict, but rather our response to inevitable conflict. Pastors sometimes complain that their churches are torn by conspiracies, conflicting factions, distrust, or unfocused anxiety. The tendency is to focus on these situations as the problem. Often they are only symptoms of the more important problem of poorly managed conflict. Time and again, when I observe a congregation in deep trouble, I feel that I am looking at a pastor and people who are paralyzed. Everyone has retreated to an armed camp. The pastor has taken refuge in some hard-and-fast "matter of principle." Such desperate situations give conflict a bad name.

"Conflict" comes from the Latin *fligere*, meaning "to strike." Conflict means, literally, "to strike together." Whenever two or more persons go after goals that they perceive to be mutually exclusive, whenever one person's needs collide with another's, conflict results. If there were no movement to fulfill ideas, goals, or desires among human beings, there would be no conflict. No movement among human beings might be defined as something like death. Thus, while conflict may not always be pleasant, the alternatives are rather stark.

The Kinds of Conflict

In order to respond to conflict more appropriately and to manage it more effectively, preachers need to know all they can about it. In their book *Church Fights,* Speed Leas and Paul Kittlaus helpfully distinguish three ways in which conflict is experienced:[1]

1. *Intrapersonal conflict:* the contest that one has when different parts of the self compete with one another. I

want to be a beloved pastor but I also want to be a preacher who speaks the truth.

2. *Interpersonal conflict:* personality differences between people that are not related primarily to issues. I like to think of myself as a strong, independent person but my administrative board chairperson treats me like an incompetent who must be told what to do.

3. *Substantive conflict:* disputes over facts, values, goals, and beliefs. I think we ought to put a new roof on the church but the social concerns committee wants to open a clothes closet for the poor.

In a given conflict in the church, there may be a mix of types of conflict. An argument over the church budget may dredge up my own doubts about my effectiveness as a pastor—substantive conflict triggers intrapersonal conflict. It is important to identify carefully what type of conflict confronts us, because different methods are appropriate for solving different kinds of conflict. Intrapersonal and interpersonal conflict, because they tend to be deeply personal and individual, can best be handled in counseling, therapy, personal confrontation, or other individualized and personal means rather than through the more public forum of the pulpit.

Honesty and self-knowledge may save a preacher from pretending that a given conflict is substantive when it is really intrapersonal. In one of my first churches I preached a sermon on the evils of wealth. I felt that my sermon was a faultless biblical diatribe against materialism in our day. On the way out of the church, a member of the board said, "Well, I bet you still want that raise, don't you, preacher?"

His comment stunned me. Earlier that month the board had struggled over next year's budget. Doubts were expressed over whether or not a pastor's salary increase would be possible. In my suppressed anger about my own salary, I had used the pulpit (abused the pulpit) as a platform for transferring my own anger about the budget to the congregation. The board member's comment showed that at least he had gotten the message: The pastor is angry and has taken the stance that, because he can't enjoy the benefits of a salary increase, no one in the congregation ought to enjoy his or her salary either!

I might have had a legitimate, substantive argument with the board about the nature of the church budget. But that was lost because of my failure to claim my own feelings about the issue. This book will focus primarily on the issue of substantive conflict and its relationship to the pulpit, since substantive conflict may sometimes be addressed in sermons. But we shall also have to admit, from time to time, how our own personal feelings and personality entanglements with others cloud our message and weaken our preaching. Sometimes an honest admission of these feelings can assist our preaching; but we shall deal with that later.

A friend of mine invested much time and energy urging his congregation to allow a community group to use the building for an interracial day care center. Gratified by the initial response of the persons with whom he discussed the issue, he urged that the board put the matter to a vote.

To his dismay, when the board discussed the issue, initial enthusiasm crumbled. Numerous objections were raised. When the vote was taken, the project was defeated. My friend was angry and hurt by the apparent timidity, backwardness, and laziness of his congregation.

"All right," he told them, "this church will be nothing but a bunch of old people. I saw this as a chance to attract some new life, but now we've blown it."

The next day, one of the faithful members came to talk to the young pastor. "I know you were angry," she said. "But you are right. We are old and we are dying. This community has changed and we have been left out of the changes. We went along with the idea of the day care center because we love you and we knew that this was your idea of what a real church does and we didn't want to risk losing you. But when it came down to the vote, we knew that we couldn't handle that day care center. We are too old, too backward, too tired—call it what you will. We wanted it only because we want you. We're sorry."

Her honesty evoked honesty in my friend. He realized that the center was his idea of the church, not theirs. He saw the center as a way of validating his ministry there: I may be stuck here in this dying little church with a bunch of old people, but at least I can boast of this day care center which validates that I am serving a real church.

At such moments pastors feel ashamed—not ashamed that they have stood in the middle of conflict but ashamed that the battle was fought for reasons having to do more with the pastor's personal needs and gratification than the pastor's commitment to the noble mission of the church. "Know thyself" is the beginning of wisdom as we wade into a church conflict and prepare to address that conflict in a sermon.

This does not mean that we should know ourselves just so that we may be better able to suppress all personal motives in order to focus more exclusively on matters of principle. A subtle process is often at work. Because the Christian faith lauds self-denial, whenever my personal feelings and needs are paramount to matters of the true, the right, and the just, something seems wrong. So we tend to say, "I'm not arguing this point because of my own feelings in the matter, this is a matter of principle."

That's often where the trouble begins. In claiming that we are arguing, not out of personal feelings, but on the basis of Christian principle alone, we idealize and dehumanize the conflict. What we have here, we tell ourselves, is not simply a disagreement among people but a clash of false faith and true faith. The issue becomes, Which side are you on? If you are not for the justice that I advocate, then you are not simply in disagreement with me, you are unjust! Thus, the attempt to eliminate the personal element tends to make conflict more bloody in the absence of modifying elements that personal factors often introduce. It is a struggle between the Children of Light versus the Children of Darkness, and we know, from even a cursory reading of history, what sort of wars that produces. The crisis rapidly escalates. I claim to be arguing not for myself but for God. This isn't what would make me happy but what would make God happy.

When, on the other hand, I am able to be honest that many of my own personal likes and dislikes shape my behavior, I am able to temper some of my demands. My motives are never pure; therefore I need not escalate my side of the conflict out of proportion to the substantive issues at stake. As a preacher who weekly bears the burden of saying something in the name of God, I am likely to be susceptible to the danger of presuming to bear the unadulterated word of truth rather than a word that is usually mixed, for good and ill, with who I am as a person. I cannot avoid being personal. In fact, I must not delude myself into thinking that such abstract, detached, pristine propositions are possible. Rather, I must assert everything with a generous dose of humility, aware, as well as anyone in the congregation, of all the ways I, to paraphrase Paul, preach myself as often as I preach Christ.

Leas and Kittlaus identify four kinds of substantive conflict:[2]

1. *Conflict over the facts* of a situation. Is there enough money to pay for the new roof?

2. *Conflict over methods or means* of achieving a solution to the problem. Should we take up a food collection for the poor in town or lobby the town council to take action on decent housing laws?

3. *Conflict over ends or goals.* Should this church be involved in direct political action or is this a matter of concern for Christian individuals alone?

4. *Conflict over values.* Values are the source of our goals and the means by which the church gains direction. Values tell us which goals are worth adopting and what means of achieving these goals is appropriately Christian. Should Christians ever be engaged in confrontation and agitation or should we always be reconcilers and peacemakers in every situation?

Conceivably, a sermon could address any of these types of substantive conflict. Is there money to pay for the new roof? What are the facts? What is the past financial history of this congregation and its present situation?

Should we lobby the town council to take action on housing? What have Christians done in the past? What action is not only most effective but also most faithful to the gospel? Who are we as a church and where do we go for help with our identity?

The acquisition of skills in diagnosing the types and the dynamics of conflict is essential for effective pastoral response to church fights. Because the pulpit is the very lifeblood of the church, the source of its identity, and the content of its witness, we preachers must exercise utmost care in our use of the pulpit as a response to church conflict.

Later in this book we shall explore specific ways the pulpit is used (and abused) in speaking to substantive disputes in the church.

Purposes of Conflict

As surprising as it may seem to peacemaking pastors, conflict has a positive role to play in the life of a congregation. In conflict, a group is energized. As an old pastor once told me, "You can put out a fire easier than you can raise the dead!" Where there is absolutely no dissatisfaction, no vision of anything better, no pain, there is little chance of action. When there is some measure of threat, individuals or groups mobilize, seek and integrate new information, and muster new skills and resources to meet the threat. A church in which there is a healthy amount of tension and conflict is a church alive.

I served a congregation where, because of our geographical situation, whenever we opened our doors, there was a constant stream of prospective members and potential new life. Yet we had a constant struggle to develop warmth, friendliness, and unity. Little interest was shown in starting new groups, visitation, and outreach. Later, I served a congregation where it was my unpleasant task to tell the members that, given the present rate of decline, we would be dead in a couple of decades because of our geographical location. The realization of that fact could have depressed and defeated the people. Fortunately it had the opposite affect. They mobilized for ministry. Visitation teams, greeters, an overhaul of the church building, and the monthly creation of new classes to meet various age and interest needs all flowed from the stark recognition that, in the words of many laypersons, "If we don't do something and don't do it quick, this church will be dead in a decade."

This suggests that a wise preacher understands that a congregation needs, even enjoys, a fair amount of tension and conflict generated from the pulpit. For everyone who complains about a "controversial" sermon, there may be two others who are just plain bored, helpless, and paralyzed because of a lack of energy within the congregation. While gratuitous and self-serving conflict for conflict's sake is an abuse of the preaching office, it is the preacher's duty to keep exposing people to the demands of scripture, to assure people that there is a force for change, for good, and for meaning in our world, and that the preacher has a vision of something better than merely present arrangements.

The more a congregation is confronted with conflict, the better the members become in handling conflict creatively. They experience themselves, not as hapless, helpless, victims of external circumstances, but as creative, resourceful persons who have been given the skills and insights they need to be the church. Accustomed to being questioned constantly about its goals and purposes, this church does not become defensive when confronted with the inevitable conflict between our ways and God's ways. Having experienced the empowerment that comes from such conflict, the church enjoys exploring ever-expanding areas of faithfulness.

Yet we must admit that there are certain parishes that are unable to bear a high level of conflict. When an individual is confronted with too much threat, his or her ability to receive and process information and perceive alternatives decreases. Rigidity sets in or breakdown occurs. What is true of individuals can also be true of groups. For instance, my friend's church, which I mentioned earlier, simply felt overwhelmed by the prospect of an interracial day care center while its members were fighting for their very survival, in danger of losing their young pastor and holding on for dear life. They felt the best they could do was to retreat and to muster what energies they had for trench warfare. If you were preaching to this congregation, what would you offer? Appeals to open themselves to change would probably fail amidst a people who were feeling utterly inundated by change. A few of their sources of fear would have to be overcome before they would have the strength to undertake new challenges. Perhaps a sermon on reassurance and strength would be more to the point than a shrill call to action.

It is my opinion that churches generally overstate their inability to handle conflict. I can think of more cases where a church was strengthened by crisis than destroyed by it. Churches are amazingly resilient. More often it is the fear of conflict that harms, the blind obedience to the notion that all conflict is wrong or unchristian that scatters people when conflict arises. Too many churches presume that the only choice they have is either no conflict or all-out war. The pastor can be the key in reassuring the members that a wide array of faithful responses are possible.

A preacher's role is more often that of opening up a congregation's vision to the wide array of faithful responses than that of narrowing everything down to the one right thing that ought to be done. The beginning of a faithful homiletical response to an apathetic church is not simply a harsh fueling of the fires but rather a firm, pastoral reassurance that this congregation really does have the resources to confront difficult circumstances rather than to suppress them. Open dealing with conflict is an affirmation of faith that the issues are worth fighting over and that we can fight over them with the reassurance that, simply because we care deeply, we shall not be destroyed.

Conflict makes all of us draw upon the resources of our faith to handle the matter at hand. Down deep, we may doubt that we have such resources. Maybe we don't. But better that such spiritual emptiness be exposed and ministered to than that it be left to fester. When a congregation has a pastor who is courageous and resourceful enough to stay and minister to people in the midst of conflict, there are few circumstances in which conflict should be suppressed and avoided. Even in a congregation's darkest hours, the Christian faith provides the resources necessary for making sense out of difficult situations and surviving them.

If we didn't really care about one another and the faith, there would be no conflict. The person who wonders why the meetings of his or her book club are more placid than those of the branch office of the kingdom of God need only measure what is at stake to understand why church fights are so fierce. If the members of a church school class have a life-and-death battle over the color of the carpet in their new room, the pastor, while chagrined at their choice of argument, at least can be pleased that they have understood that their involvement in the church is a matter of life and death.

Where a congregation operates on a style of constant suppression of conflict, conflict acts like a pressure cooker. The heat continues to build; the inevitable explosion is more destructive. Through continuous release of pressure in the weekly struggles of an open, active parish, conflict is less likely to be destructive. When conflict is constantly suppressed, it tends to explode in the most unlikely ways over the most unlikely issues. It appears more baffling than ever, and great energy is required to deal with what appears to be an irrational blowup over a petty issue. As Leas and Kittlaus say, "Conflict properly managed is conflict continually managed."[3]

Conflict Potential

Wise management of conflict begins with pastoral sensitivity to potential for conflict. Jesus urged his disciples to discern the signs of the times: a fig tree blossoming, a storm cloud gathering. Discerning potential conflict is both an intuitional and a rational matter. Experienced pastors who have weathered conflict in the past often become better able to diagnose conflict in the present. Yet, in spite of conventional wisdom, experience is not always the best teacher. Experience means little if we have no framework for learning from experience, for enabling ministry to be more than a simple meandering from one collision to the next. Some pastors always seem to be in the midst of conflict. Many of them like to think it is because they are particularly "prophetic" or "outspoken." Often their troubles stem from simple incompetence or personality problems of their own which have little to do with the substantive issues of the gospel.

Aside from whatever intuitional gifts we may have been given or experience we may have gained, there are some guides that can help us to diagnose conflict potential within a congregation. Every congregation is an ecological system in which conflict will be treated in certain ways. A pastor cannot assume that, simply because the last church found it easy to deal with controversy, the present congregation will be able to do so. Congregations deal with conflict on the basis of their assumptions about conflict. Assumptions arise from a host of factors: What has been the congregation's experience with conflict in the past? Has past conflict led to growth or to retrenchment and fear? What congregational folklore emerges when conflict arises? Colloquial expressions such as "Let sleeping dogs lie" or "Don't open up that can of worms" reveal underlying assumptions. What is the group's capacity for making changes in their situation? Age, sex, educational level, and attitudinal flexibility all affect our ability to deal with conflict. When people have been hurt previously by conflict, they fear and avoid it. The more painful the past experience has been, the more cautious the pastor must be in handling the present conflict.

As we indicated earlier, conflict is a sign of vitality. It occurs most often in congregations in which there is a deep commitment to the church. People only fight over what is important to them. Of course, not all church fights are over issues of theological substance, but all church fights are potentially revelatory of what is important to the combatants.

The youth go on a retreat to the beach and, while there, hear a controversial speaker. When they return home and tell their parents, a furious controversy erupts in the church over the leadership of the youth program. The pastor begins by trying to find out what the speaker said. The speaker was discussing premarital sex. Thus, the pastor assumes that the controversy must be over proper Christian attitudes about sex. However, the more deeply the pastor investigates the conflict, the more he is led to conclude that the real issue at stake, the real cause of the conflict, is the fear of the parents that they may be losing their influence over their children. The parents expect the church to be a means of helping them control the lives and behavior of their children. If it fails to do this, then the church's entire youth program is a failure. What are we really fighting over? is a fundamental question to raise in any church conflict.

The structure of a congregation is another source of potential conflict. How is the church organized? Pastors sometimes speak of a "family church," a church in which a prominent family makes all the important decisions and passes church offices around to family members. Sometimes a church is divided between the "new" and the "old" members, such as a church in a transitional neighborhood. Or there may be constant competition, and thus constant conflict, between various factions or committees or groups in the church.

The environment of a congregation is yet another source of conflict. Few congregations have control over the neighborhood or environment in which they find themselves; yet it is a decisive factor. The local steel plant closes and a congregation that once had the human and financial resources to accomplish any task finds itself in a depressed condition.

Paul says that you and I bear a "treasure in earthen vessels" (2 Cor. 4:7). The glory of the gospel is contained in a thoroughly human community. Conflict is a reminder, often a painful one, that the body of Christ is still tied to the facts of the human condition as it strives to be all that God calls it to be. Even as the Word had to become flesh to enter into the conflicts that beset the human condition, so the church must be willing to enter into the vortex of conflict in order to be a part of God's act of reconciliation in the world. As preachers, we are called to be ministers of reconciliation, a vocation that cannot be fulfilled without fulfilling it in conflict. In the next chapter we shall examine some of the things preachers must consider before speaking to congregational problems from the pulpit.

2

What's Going On Here?

Fight or flee? Are not these the basic human instincts that enable our species to survive? Whenever a pastor is faced with congregational conflict, there are two choices. The pastor can ignore the situation or can intervene. Ignoring the situation means that the conflict will either go away or get worse. I once worked with a pastor who felt that one should not respond to conflict within the parish until there was absolutely no way of continuing to avoid it. He would never have considered dragging some problem into the pulpit or giving voice to a problem on his own initiative. Hear no evil, speak no evil, was his homiletical philosophy. I was surprised how many problems seemed to resolve themselves if one just simply sat back and let things run their course. As time moved on, I discovered that a number of problems that we assumed had been resolved had simply become submerged or channeled in another direction, only to rear their ugly heads on the least expected occasions. In other words, ignoring the conflict did not solve anything. The conflict simmered until it bubbled over, often doing much more long-term damage than it would have if we had confronted it directly.

Even so, there is such a thing as creative avoidance of crisis. Most ministers learn that one must choose one's battles. If a pastor reacts to every potentially conflicted situation, ministry will degenerate into a frantic attempt to be everywhere at once, doing everything for everybody. Pastoral work will become diffused over too wide an area. Relatively minor hassles will be conflated into major confrontations, so that the pastor is constantly bogged down in crisis. But there is a difference between ignoring conflict and avoiding conflict. What the wise pastor wants is the ability to guide and to impact potentially conflicted situations without allowing them to become conflicts that are destructive to parish life.

There is a leadership style whereby the pastor keeps alert for developing conflict and then acts to influence the results of a conflict between persons. Avoidance can be part of this style if the pastor responds before the conflict has become a public encounter. Some avoidance is simply denial of conflict, withdrawal in silence and nothing more. As we noted earlier, this type of avoidance will probably make matters worse. When we merely ignore conflict, we are only confessing our ignorance. Ignorance is not a helpful leadership quality. Creative avoidance seeks appropriate ways to move potential conflict into the public arena whereby the factors that are leading the congregation toward conflict may be examined, discussed, reflected upon, and redirected toward possible reconciliation.

Assessing Conflict

Here are some steps for assessing potential conflict in its earliest stages:

1. *Obtain as much information as possible about the potential conflict.* Many church conflicts are the result of poor communication or misinformation. This initial step is a relatively nonthreatening gesture toward the parties of the conflict whereby one is only seeking better understanding of what is at stake.

2. *Buy as much time as possible.* When people are under pressure to reach a quick decision, there is little time to work out differences and seek alternatives. Delay is a means of avoidance whereby time is gained to function wisely.

3. *Make an assessment of the individuals involved in the potential conflict.* How mature are they? Is this merely the work of isolated, chronic troublemakers, people who, because of some purely personal reason, are trying to create a congregational crisis where none exists? Pastors are

sometimes quick to label people as troublemakers in order to avoid coming to terms with legitimate differences within the congregation, so we must take care in our diagnosis. However, there are people in every congregation whose level of personal need is so high that they seem to thrive on the creation of conflict. These persons should be identified by the pastor and offered individual care.

4. *Take the emotional temperature of the conflict at this point.* Anger can build quickly in conflict and counteract the pastor's attempts to deal with the conflict in a rational manner. If the anger is at a high level, what can the pastor do to initiate a cooling-off period? Humor, distraction into some other activity for the time being, or simple delay can be helpful means of bringing the emotions generated by the conflict down to more manageable levels.

These steps can be helpful before conflict reaches the boiling point and becomes public within the congregation. But once the conflict surfaces, a different set of strategies will be needed. Before conflict attains public dimensions, it can often be dealt with relatively quietly in a committee meeting, through a conference of the participants, or in counseling with the pastor. After a conflict is made public, it is pointless for the pastor to continue to act as if nothing is happening. Many pastors have a relatively passive leadership style. They feel that they will ensure a passive congregational life by continuing to go about with a smile on the face, slapping people on the back jovially, and denying that there is a problem. But when a problem becomes public, the passive style merely indicates to the congregation that the pastor has lost control and either is unwilling or unable to intervene in a constructive way. When conflict becomes public, the pastor must actively respond. How?

Pastoral Strategies for Congregational Conflict

The choice of response will be determined by an assessment of which strategy would be most helpful in moving the persons in conflict toward constructive growth or resolution. Fear, denial, and all-out war are rarely constructive.

In their book *Conflict Ministry in the Church,* Larry McSwain

and William Treadwell suggest that the first step, once conflict has become a public matter within the congregation, is
diffusion. [4] Diffusion is effective particularly when the conflict
has taken the congregation as a whole by surprise or when
it seems to be concentrated within a small group. When this
happens, use the following steps:

1. Be sure that everyone in the group knows the facts
of the situation. Healthy decision-making cannot occur
until everyone understands. One faction must not be allowed to pressure everyone else into a quick decision
before all parties have had the opportunity to be in-
formed about the issues.

2. Ask someone to explain the history of the conflict.
The current situation is probably the result of a complex
of factors that may have a long history. Most conflicts are
presented as relatively simple matters requiring the taking of a stand. They are rarely simple, once the whole
history of the crisis is known.

3. Refer the conflict to the proper committee for discussion and recommendation. When conflicts emerge in
a large group, they must not be discussed there but must
quickly be moved to a smaller forum. Often the conflict
is the result of the personal agenda of some individual
and that personal agenda can best be confronted in a
smaller body.

4. Enlarge the conflicted group with persons who can
help move the group to a constructive engagement.
Sometimes small committees become deadlocked and
dysfunctional. By drawing new life into the group, old
alliances can be broken and new insights can be given.

5. Delay action until there has been time to attempt to
manage the conflict. In fact, to a certain degree, all the
above steps are means of delaying a decision about the
conflict until a proper analysis can occur.

Having diffused the conflict, the group is better able to
move into what McSwain and Treadwell call the *problem-
solving analysis,* the phase whereby the group is moved to a
decision:[5]

1. Collect all facts, feelings, and opinions about the
conflict.

2. List the various options to the problem, including the potential results of using each option and all the positive and negative consequences.

3. List each option in the order of priority. Which option apparently involves the fewest negative consequences?

4. Depersonalize the options. We must remind ourselves that we are not voting on the personalities of the persons involved in the conflict.

5. Develop a consensus of a group support for the option that most nearly resolves the conflict. Compromise may be required for us to have consensus.

Preaching as a Strategy

Where does preaching fit into all of this? We have explored the nature of conflict in order better to understand the dynamics that may be operative during congregational crises. No word can be heard from the pulpit or anywhere else that is not applicable to the specific situation of the hearer.

Preaching is best thought of as the part of a total pastoral response to congregational conflict. It is not the only or necessarily the most effective pastoral response, because the nature of the conflict will determine whether or not preaching should be used to minister to the conflict. But preaching is among the legitimate pastoral responses in times of congregational conflict.

At times, preaching may best function early in the development of the conflict. For instance, a pastor hears rumblings that some persons in the congregation are unhappy with the denomination's stance on labor unions. Some have suggested that the congregation ought to consider withholding a portion of its contribution to the denomination because of their disagreement over the issue. Before the issue is formally discussed, the pastor decides to preach a sermon that will deal with the church's responsibility to speak on social issues, perhaps using the issue of organized labor as an example. In the sermon the pastor will mention briefly the denomination's long history of social involvement, including involvement in the issue of organized labor. The sermon's intention will be to offer information that can be used by the congregation in a future consideration of this issue.

At other times, the sermon might attempt to channel the movement of the conflict away from personalities toward issues by analyzing brewing conflict and conceptualizing its nature so that participants begin focusing on concepts rather than on personalities. One congregation experienced growing tension between the older members who had lived in the neighborhood for many years and younger members who had recently moved into the neighborhood. The pastor noted increasing references to "the old guard" and "the newcomers." In a sermon, the pastor noted that every family needs young and old in order to enrich the family. The church, the family of God, is no exception. So the issue is not whether we will be a church for older people or a church for younger people. The issue is, How can our church develop its mission, its internal programs, and life together in such a way that it becomes a diverse, rich, many-faceted congregation? The preacher hoped that his sermon would help members to conceptualize the issues better and avoid an unproductive conflict in which people simply chose up sides on the basis of age or longevity within the congregation rather than on the basis of a given issue under consideration.

In later chapters we will discuss specific problems and possibilities involved in speaking to conflict from the pulpit. For now, let us note that we need to build upon the insights from studies of conflict management in any attempt to address conflict as Christian preachers.

When conflicts become ugly within a congregation, there are usually a number of common characteristics of the crisis. The problem has become a we-they confrontation rather than a matter of we versus the problem. All energies are directed toward total victory or total defeat, with little room for compromise. Each party sees things from its own point of view rather than as a mutual dilemma. Everything is directed toward a solution rather than toward definition of goals, values, and motives to be attained. Instead of focusing on facts and issues, conflicts are personalized. The parties in the dispute are conflict-oriented, emphasizing immediate disagreement rather than relationship orientation, emphasizing the long-term effect of differences and how they are resolved. The question for the homiletician is, How will my sermon minister to this conflict and related conditions whereby these destructive tendencies might be overcome?[6]

One fundamental reason why congregations are plagued by conflict is that there is no consensus within the congregation about the purpose and nature of the church. In today's mobile society, where half the population moves every five years, many congregations are faced with the task of continually integrating newcomers into the congregation. Preaching, as a major source of Christian identity, is the chief opportunity for reiterating the stories, values, and visions that make a congregation Christian. Through this process the community gathers and focuses itself, celebrates its common goals, and underscores its mission. All of this is to suggest that much of our preaching, while not specifically related to solving a particular conflict within the congregation, is essential preparation for the Christian resolution of conflicts when they occur. A congregation that has no center, no general consensus about the direction of the church, is ill equipped to handle crisis. Thus the preaching that occurs in a congregation, week in and week out, is a major component in conflict management.

Pastoral Styles in Conflict Management

Finally, as we are assessing the various factors involved in a congregational conflict, taking the emotional temperature of the situation, gathering information, planning strategies, and thinking about a sermon on the crisis at hand, let us remind ourselves that we are responding to the crisis as persons who have our own hidden goals, feelings, and attitudes. Preaching is a very personal endeavor, and so is conflict management. Each one of us has a distinct homiletical style in the pulpit which is developed from our personality. This style will stamp our ministry in general, even as it puts an indelible mark on our sermons.

In the midst of a conflict, our style will be evident. We tend to use the same style, regardless of the nature of the conflict. When we are preaching, we learn that some styles elicit certain kinds of response from our listeners. If we want a sermon to convey graciousness, then we try not to preach the text in a way that conveys anger. Laypersons sometimes complain that, regardless of the biblical text being treated in a given sermon, their preacher always sounds the same. The texts change, but not the preacher's style. What is your predominant style?

McSwain and Treadwell identify five styles that ministers often utilize as they confront (or avoid!) conflict within their parishes.

The Problem Solver. The problem solver refuses to deny or to flee the conflict. This type of pastor keeps pressing for conversation and negotiation of the conflict until a satisfactory conclusion is reached. Paul confronted a major problem in the early church—food shortages in Jerusalem. He proposed that a large collection be taken from the more affluent Gentile congregations. The money would meet the physical needs of those in Jerusalem and, at the same time, also address the problem of Gentile Christians, showing them that the other Christians welcomed them, even without circumcision. He decided to address the conflict by circulating a letter (sermon?) among the churches in which he called them to follow Christ's example in giving (2 Corinthians 8–9). In Romans 15:14–29 he further developed the theological rationale for such a collection. An intrachurch problem was thus an occasion for Paul to proclaim the gospel in a new and challenging way.

The problem-solver style is an effective way of addressing conflict. It is most effective in those situations in which communication problems are at the heart of the conflict and where the group shares common goals. One of the main tasks of the problem solver is to help participants verbalize conflict in depersonalized ways. In the sermon, a preacher helps the participants find words that will give them the means of grasping the problem and seeking alternative solutions.

Because the problem solver does not fear conflict, he or she can be most helpful to a conflict-laden congregation. However, there are weaknesses in this pastoral style. Emotionally explosive situations are sometimes beyond the problem-solving approach. People are simply too angry for the dispassionate deliberation required. Settings in which there is deep conflict between goals also undercut the work of the problem solver. There is the additional weakness that the problem solver may be so intent on moving everyone along to the solution that he or she overlooks other important dynamics. There will be exasperation with those intransigent people who refuse to be moved toward a solution.

I remember reading a book some years ago that advocated constructing sermons by seeing every biblical text as a problem to be solved. The preacher states the problem posed by the text: How could this happen? Why on earth would Jesus have said this? What are we supposed to do with this commandment?

Then, in the sermon, the preacher moves to a solution of the problem. A major difficulty is that this method forces into a mold a great many biblical texts that in no way attempt to pose a "problem." They want to instruct, to encourage, to edify, to condemn, to envision.

The problem-solver pastor is in danger of forgetting that resolving disputes is only one part of pastoral work. The pastor, like the biblical texts that guide the church, must often instruct, encourage, edify, condemn, and envision. The preacher is more than a mere manager of conflict. People are more significant than mere problems to be solved. Many of humanity's most basic conflicts will not be solved as long as we are on this earth, and the gospel has a word to speak to those conflicts too, a word that transcends mere solutions. Can the problem-solver minister to people even when solutions are not found?

The Super Helper. The super helper is constantly working to help others, with little thought for self. This person is the "messiah," often passive in conflicts involving self but quite involved in assisting others as they work through their conflicts. Since pastors are expected to be long-suffering, compassionate, and always willing to help, many super helpers will be attracted to this vocation.

The super helper is not always a good conflict minister. By being so concerned with others, he or she may ignore personal needs for self-support. His or her own physical, emotional, and spiritual health may be neglected in the intense desire (or need) to love others. The possible anger or frustration of the super helper goes unacknowledged and unleashed. Burnout is too often the result.

In a conflict, the super helper will feel a sense of failure if all parties in the dispute are not happy with the achieved solution. The super helper will tend to take on too much responsibility for group problems, feeling that it is personally up to him or her to set everything right rather than assisting the congregation itself to set things right. Once again, there are many conflicts that do not lend themselves to painless solutions. Those conflicts will cause the super helper much anguish.

The Power Broker. The power broker uses whatever power is available to resolve a conflict. The power broker is committed to winning, because power tends to transform us all into winners or losers. There are many conflicts where the differences in substantive conflict are so contradictory that mutually inclusive goals are not possible. Only power can solve the crisis. For instance, a church cannot be racially inclusive and exclusive at the same time. Any resolution of this problem will involve someone feeling like a winner and someone feeling like a loser.

For the power broker, solutions are more important than relationships. If someone leaves the church as the result of the solution, this is unfortunate but not devastating to the power broker, because a solution was achieved. In the eyes of the power broker, it is important for the pastor to "hang tough" in many situations, to assert that "the buck stops here" and that "if you can't stand the heat, get out of the kitchen." Some congregations seem to thrive under the leadership of a power broker. They must be willing to give the pastor or a lay group major decision-making power. Congregations that value participatory democracy in governance will be unhappy with the power-broker style.

The major liability of this style is that, when the power broker fails to motivate the congregation to do what he or she thinks best, the power broker resorts to manipulation. Having a high level of confidence in his or her own insights and abilities, the power broker has little room for the opinions of others. Those who dare to challenge the direction of the power broker will often be isolated or driven from the fellowship. Followers are what the power broker needs, not colleagues or fellow workers.

The Facilitator. The facilitator is highly adaptive to a variety of situations and styles in order to achieve a compromise between competing factions. Acts 15 presents James as just such a leader in the controversy over the Gentile mission in

Antioch. He moved into a tense situation with a spirit of conciliation and proposed a solution that appealed to both sides in the battle.

Compromise tends to be most effective as a style of leadership where differences are attitudinal or emotional. If there are substantive differences, participants will be angered by the attempts of the facilitator to move everyone to some benign middle ground where they can all agree on everything. The facilitator will be regarded as a weak-principled peacemaker who is always trying to suppress real ideological differences in order to keep everyone happy.

In congregations where there is a plurality of factions, ministers often become facilitators so that things can be held together in the absence of consensus on congregational goals and values. The facilitator is similar to the problem solver, but the facilitator is less sure that the group has the resources to be honest about its differences and to manage them effectively, so the facilitator seeks peace more than solutions. In the face of a major disruption, the facilitator is prone to become passive and fearful that "things will blow wide open" and disintegrate.

The facilitator style risks keeping a congregation in a constant spirit of compromise and even suppressing conflict rather than allowing conflict to move the congregation to a new level of consensus. The lowest common denominator of agreement is sought rather than a truly creative solution. The laity become confused or even angry because their pastor seems willing to support a wide array of mutually exclusive positions. Always seeking the middle ground, the pastor may be perceived not as a peacemaker but as one without conviction, a weak leader who is ultimately unhelpful for the long-term growth of the congregation.

The Fearful Loser. The fearful loser runs from conflict. Quiet and retiring in personal behavior, the fearful loser finds that conflict produces intense personal insecurity. The congregation senses this, and if the members are charitable, they suppress all conflict (or move conflict underground) in order to protect their fragile pastor. When the conflict bubbles up and demands to be acknowledged, the fearful loser is likely to resign and move elsewhere, hoping to find the perfect conflict-free congregation. Because the fearful loser must suppress not only congregational conflict but also his or her own personal feelings, constant compliance and passivity eventually produce hostility. The pastor blames the congregation for unduly restricting him or her, while the congregation impatiently waits for the pastor finally to stand up and take charge. At the root of the fearful loser's problem is his or her own painfully low self-image and lack of confidence. Conflicts cannot be engaged because the pastor perceives himself or herself as a loser, unable positively to speak a word of wisdom to the conflict.

Which description best fits your style of ministry? Most pastors are probably some of each, some of the time. Undoubtedly, the positive, self-assured, trusting style of the problem solver is the most ideal for most parish conflict. So we pause now for a moment of honest self-evaluation before we move into an exploration of the ways in which our preaching is a resource in our management of church conflict. Who am I as I move into conflict? What is my style? How does my congregation perceive me in the pulpit and in the committee meeting? How can I become more aware of who I am so that I might minister more effectively? As Paul says, to us has been given "the ministry of reconciliation . . . entrusting to us the message of reconciliation" (2 Cor. 5:18–19). It is to the method and the means of that reconciliation that we now turn.

3

To Speak or Not to Speak

In the book of Acts, we are told that the Spirit descended upon people "from every nation under heaven" (Acts 2:5), enabling each person to hear and understand every other person, so that "all who believed were together and had all things in common" (Acts 2:44).

But Luke's picture of primal harmony is more of a goal than an accurate description of the way things really were in the early church. Paul says, "When you assemble as a church, I hear that there are divisions among you; and I partly believe it" (1 Cor. 11:18). Christ calls all to be part of his kingdom, but because of the inclusiveness of that kingdom, because of its high goals and difficult tasks, conflict is inevitable.

Because of the potential for conflict in the church, the ordained ministry emerged during the first centuries of the church. Early congregations designated leaders to help in the task of edifying the people of God. The ordained ministry exists for no other reason than to help the church to be the church. Elsewhere, I have spoken of pastors as "community persons."[7] The church asks its pastors to lead in forming the community as well as prompting the community to criticize dimensions of the faith. All Christians are called to witness, to serve, to grow in faith. But some Christians, the clergy, are called for the additional task of edifying the church. Pastors will therefore focus on the presence of inequality, division, and diversity within the congregation. They will, in their pastoral work, seek to foster a climate where consensus and reconciliation will occur; to judge the potentially demonic aspects of cheerful "togeth-erness"; to ask whether the community sought is a specifi-cally Christian community; to distinguish between their personal preferences and what the congregation's cohesion requires. The pastor is, to use a very ancient term for church officials, a *pontifex* (literally, "bridge builder") for the congregation, the one who is constantly building bridges between rich and poor, insiders and outsiders, young and old in the congregation.

By What Authority?

All of this is to underscore that, when a pastor addresses congregational crises, he or she is doing so under the au-thority of the church. The pastor is there because of certain things that the community needs done. A primary task that needs doing in the church is the building of a community worthy of the gospel. Admittedly, the presence of the priest or pastor does not guarantee community. But his or her presence does guarantee a visible, personal reminder that, in the church, common concerns are paramount to individ-ual ones. Other fellow Christians may chiefly concern them-selves with their own struggle as individual Christians. But the focus of the pastor is upon the communal expression of the faith.

The burden of the ordained ministry is that priests and pastors have the vantage point from where they can get a firsthand view of the lack of community within the congre-gation, the difficulties of achieving real unity, and the divi-sions within the church they serve. The pastor may feel deeply troubled by the apparent inability of the congrega-tion to look like the "real" church. The pastor's disappoint-ment over the inability of the congregation to achieve unity is itself evidence that the pastor is in the middle of what the church needs most from its leaders: aid in the struggle out of pastors' rugged individualism toward gospel-promised community.

There are pastors who resist this communally bestowed authority. They will chafe at the designation of themselves as "priest" or "pastor." Instead, they like to think of them-selves more modestly, as "enabler" or "facilitator," a good friend standing in the wings urging the laity to be the church. Their modesty is inappropriate to the ordained ministry, arising more often from their own need to avoid ministering to the real needs of the congregation than from their feigned sense of humility. Leadership is not an optional matter for any group, particularly a group like the church which is called to such difficult tasks. The authority for ministry is a gift, bestowed upon us by the church in order that the church might be the church. One can exercise authority without being authoritarian—Jesus noted the difference between Gentile leaders who enjoyed lording over their subjects and the leadership style he urged upon his disciples. But there is no way of avoiding the need for skilled, appropriate leadership.

Most church observers agree that the quality of the relationship between the leaders and the members of a congregation is the single most important factor in the health of a congregation. As a voluntary association, parish leadership tends to be far more political than managerial. That is, clergy must build consensus among the people whom they would lead. Churches sometimes copy the managerial style of planning, goal-setting, and evaluation that characterizes corporations. This managerial style usually ends in boredom and a dispirited congregation led by clergy who have forgotten the peculiar nature of the church and their roles. Clergy do not have the coercive powers of an employer. All they have is whatever consensus they are able to forge by their own leadership.

New pastors go through what is sometimes called "the honeymoon" stage. More accurately, what feels like "the honeymoon" is really the probationary period. This is a time of mutual testing, mutual probing. If the congregation finds that the pastor is a person who is trustworthy, then the stage is set for the first real crisis. How well will this new pastor function when the congregation most needs a leader?

A new pastor will find that a pastor's power is a far more complex matter than simply the bestowal of authority at the time of ordination. A pastor's influence over a congregation must be authenticated during various stages, and their accompanying crises, within the congregation. An older pastor once commented, "It takes one difficult funeral before you become their pastor." What I heard him saying was that it takes at least one difficult crisis, in which the people have an opportunity to see the new pastor function, before they authenticate and trust his or her leadership.

In preaching to congregational crises, the pastor realizes that more is at stake here than simply finding a workable solution. Pastoral leadership is the result of interaction between members and their pastor. This crisis will be a test of her or his authenticity as a leader. The people must give authority to the pastor before she or he can minister to them. All of this means that the pastoral relationship with the people may be at stake in how well the pastor is able to speak to this crisis. The people are listening, wondering if the word they will hear will confirm that this person is indeed their community's person or if they must wait for a word from another.

Thus, in standing up to speak to a crisis in the congregation, the pastor is not going on an ego trip or flexing his or her clerical muscle, the pastor is engaged in humble, but utterly necessary service for the community. Let us be honest: We pastors often avoid speaking to various crises and conflicts, not because we are concerned that we might inappropriately dominate others, but because it is easier to avoid a conflict than to confront it. Standing in the wings, prompting the laity to settle the dispute alone, we feel that at least we are not center stage where, when the play is a flop, the disaster will be blamed on us.

Why Do We Preach?

Even if we grant that a pastor has the authority to oversee and encourage the unity of the congregation, why should a pastor think of the sermon as the proper place to minister to a congregational crisis?

Anthropologists indicate that an individual becomes human through learning language. There are experiences that one cannot know before there are words for them. Just as a person becomes a person by learning language, so we become Christian by hearing and enacting the language that speaks of Christ. A Buddhist and a Christian differ, in great part, because they have learned two very different "languages," two dissimilar stories. Language forms a world, a culture, in which certain things are valued and others are not. I once heard that the Eskimos have twenty different words for what I call "snow." Presumably, because of all these words, when an Eskimo looks at snow he or she sees much more than I see.

Religion is the long process of being socialized and enculturated into ways of seeing, speaking, and living. To be a Christian is to be someone who allows his or her situation to be molded by the biblical stories that stretch from creation to Jesus' passion and resurrection. By listening to the stories of Jesus, we are formed into certain sorts of people who live in the world in a certain way. The biblical story begins to define our being, our values, our aspirations.

It is the preacher's task continually to bring the congregation into contact with that formative story, confident that in this story is the source of our life. Week in and week out, preachers struggle to allow the church's book to speak through their sermons. If preachers always take their cue from contemporary events, the latest congregational crisis, or the personal needs of individual members, their sermons degenerate into mere therapy, politics, or the mirroring of contemporary concerns and conventional solutions—something less than the gospel. If, on the other hand, preachers simply restate scripture without reference to the present struggles of the faith community to be faithful to that scripture, their sermons are little more than dry lectures on ancient history—interesting perhaps, but detached from the life-and-death struggle that exists between God's word and God's people.

When Paul was confronted with an ugly situation of hostility and divisions in First Church Corinth, he could have responded in a variety of ways. He could have told the Corinthians, "Obey your leaders. Do what they tell you to do and stop all this bickering." Or he could have said, "People like you are a disgrace to the church and ought to burn in hell because of your pettiness."

Instead, Paul decided to pick up on the images of baptism as grafting onto a body, in the same way that a tree may be grafted in order to produce better fruit. He says, "For just as the body is one and has many members, and all the members of the body, though many, are one body, so it is with Christ. For by one Spirit we were all baptized into one body—Jews or Greeks, slaves or free—and all were made to drink of one Spirit" (1 Cor. 12:12–13).

This early preacher reminds his congregation of the story—they have all been baptized, they have all been made to drink from the same cup. Therefore they have been or are being transformed from diverse and bickering individualists to one body in the one Spirit. We see this same pattern—of remembrance, image-making, and proclamation—in countless instances throughout scripture.

The preacher decides to minister to a congregational problem through the sermon because, in the preacher's judgment, this is an appropriate intersection between the church and its book. The Bible exists, not as a detached collection of various religious thoughts, but as specific response, of the faith community's leaders, to contemporary crises within the faith community. That is why our biblical interpretation is often so difficult. Hermeneutics would be a simple matter if the Bible were merely a conglomeration of poetic thoughts on various inspirational subjects. But the Bible is doing business with timely concerns of that faith community at a particular time and place. So we must first determine, at least to some degree, what was the nature of the crisis that occasioned this particular response in the Bible before we can begin to discern a word for our own time and place.

Some years ago I was serving a church that was having problems with divisions among various groups within the congregation. When I arrived at the church, I was told, "This is a family church. The Joneses think that nobody can be an officer or teach Sunday school except a Jones. The Smiths think that, just because they own half the county, that entitles them to run everything here. You will eventually need to decide whether you are to be a preacher to the Smiths or the Joneses."

One could see the factionalism in the congregation just by observing where everyone sat in the Sunday service. The Joneses sat toward the rear on the right. The Smiths sat on the left. Although some new residents in the community had visited our church, we had little hope of growth as long as the church was so divided.

It was Pentecost, the birthday of the church, so this

seemed like an appropriate Sunday to address the problem
of divisions. I looked at the assigned lessons. Of course, the
familiar Pentecost lesson is Acts 2, the story of the Pen-
tecostal descent of the Spirit in Jerusalem. With all the
nations present at Pentecost, the Spirit descended and the
church was empowered for unity and witness.

The lesson from the Hebrew scriptures was the well
known but not so frequently preached story of the tower of
Babel. My opinion of this text had not changed much since
I first studied it in seminary: here was a typical Genesis
account of the consequences of human pride.

But further study of Genesis 11:1–11, under the guidance
of Walter Brueggemann's fine commentary on Genesis,
convinced me that this ancient story was more complex and
interesting than I first had thought and that it might relate
to the problems of unity and community at our church. We
were suffering from the problems of a divided faith community. The people in Genesis 11 were suffering from a problem of a divided faith community. They had the same
language, which gave them unity. They did not want to be
"scattered," so they decided to take matters into their own
hands in order to preserve their unity. They built a great
tower in order to unify themselves. Here, in part, is what I
said in my sermon about the tower of Babel story and its
relationship to the need for unity in our church. The title
of my sermon was "Let's Get Together."

*   *   *

My, look what happened while God was away! The last
time God took a little time off, Adam and Eve got into
trouble in the garden. Now, a little later, people are better
organized and even more rebellious. The earlier trouble
began when man and woman got together and decided to
take matters into their own hands. You know that story.

There are many more of them. The heirs of Adam and
Eve have gotten organized. There was only one language
then, and just a few words. And what were their first words?
"Come, let us build ourselves a city, and a tower with its top
in the heavens, and let us make a name for ourselves, lest
we be scattered abroad upon the face of the whole earth."

Here is the first instance of global cooperation—the fore-
runner of the UN, the multinational corporation, the World

Council of Churches, the first Family Night Covered-Dish Supper. Come, let's get together and do something significant.

God has said to humanity, "Be fruitful and multiply." Human beings are to spread throughout all the earth (Gen. 1:28). After the Flood, God made a promise with humanity, blessing all creatures and letting them be partners in God's work. The story of humanity got off to a bad start, what with Adam and Eve and Cain and Abel, but now, after the Flood, God makes a fresh beginning and we hope for something better.

But humanity becomes enlightened. "Come, let us build ourselves a city, and a tower with its top in the heavens, and let us make a name for ourselves, lest we be scattered."

The key to understanding this old story is the word "scatter." Humankind realizes that it is in danger of being scattered. So the people launch the first model cities program in order to unify themselves. But God will have none of their unity. The story ends with God scattering "them abroad over the face of all the earth" (Gen. 11:9).

It's a story about scattering. Humanity fears scattering and takes action to prevent it. But God, against the will of humanity, scatters. Is "scattering" God's punishment for presumptuous humanity? In some biblical passages, scatter can refer to exile. But in Genesis, "spreading abroad" (Gen. 10:32) is the being fruitful and multiplying that God expects of humanity.

Humanity's fear of scattering is resistance to God's purposes for creation. The people do not wish to spread abroad and fill the earth. They want to stay in their own safe havens of homogeneity. The tower of Babel and the city are attempts at self-serving unity which resists God's scattering activity.

I can understand your resistance to such an interpretation. As Christians we tend to view unity as God's purpose. But the story of Babel suggests that there are at least two kinds of unity. The unity willed by God is that all humanity should be in relationship with God and with God only, responding to God's purposes, relying upon God's power.

The scattering that God wills is that the earth should be peopled everywhere by God's agents, who are attentive to every corner of creation.

But we prefer to carve out our own destiny, just as we did back in the garden, just like the time Cain picked up a rock and killed Abel. We don't want to be scattered. We would rather huddle together in our "community." Different languages, races, families, and colors and kinds of people are viewed by us as some sort of divine punishment, something that we must labor to overcome, a threat to humanity's ability to consolidate its own power. If we don't get ourselves together and do something about all these confusing, messy, differences, we will be left vulnerable, weak, and dependent. We might have to rely on some other power greater than our own, and then where would we be?

But what if these differences, which cause us so many problems, are part of God's will, a means of ensuring that all humanity might look to and respond to God for its unity? And that, I think, is the point of this old story of the tower of Babel.

Here is a story about ill-gotten human unity as opposed to the unity that God wills—a unity centered only upon God's will for humanity. God has told human beings to scatter. But they don't want to scatter. They want to stay where they are, in their own little community of common language, common race, and common place. If we can just get everybody to talk with the same accent, wear the same clothes, believe the same slogans, and work on the same common projects, we can make a name for ourselves—we can all get together and be as great as God without God.

The story says that there are at least two ways to solve the problem of our diversity and differences: community organized around what we want or community formed on the basis of what God wants.

What we want is community based on our definitions of people like us. Like attracts like. That's what some of the proponents of the church growth movement say. If you want your church to grow, make sure your church is homogeneous, full of people like yourselves.

Didn't Jesus say, "Go therefore and make disciples of all nations"? Didn't he say to his first disciples, "You guys scatter"? Well, yes. But we had better put down stakes here, get our building paid for by keeping the church middle-class, middle-aged, middle of the road, full of people like us.

God wants us to scatter. We want unity, community, on

our terms. Let's all join hands with people like us and we can create a community so secure, so unified, so strong that we won't need God. Our striving for community can be demonic—national solidarity, racial purity, the fatherland.

The story of Babel suggests that the unity sought by fearful humanity is organized as defense against the purposes of God. Failing to trust God's plans for humanity, we fall back on "community" based on language, sex, race, class, nation, or family name. It is the unity of the fortress mentality, in which we seek to construct some tower—a smokestack, a space shuttle, a church, a capital, a business— any tower will do, which frees us from the demands of the living God. It is unity grounded in fear and meaninglessness. Such unity, the story suggests, is ultimately in vain.

So it's a story about what kind of community we will have, about whether or not we shall be organized for God's purposes. The scattering into all the world which arose from God's promise to love us and use us, wherever we are, becomes our curse of scattered languages, warring nations, competing families, divided sexes and humanity, babbling but nobody hearing or listening, and stumbles into a confused future. It's a sad story.

But it is not the only story. One day, long after Babel, it was the day of Pentecost. People "from every nation under heaven" were gathered "in one place"—Parthians talking to Parthians, Elamites huddling with Elamites, Phrygianese speaking to Phrygianese, Libyans with Libyans, Egyptians with Egyptians. Everybody was sticking with his or her own kind.

And the Spirit of God descended like wildfire. Suddenly, they heard. They understood. They couldn't believe their ears.

"What does this mean?" they asked.

"It means that you're drunk," babbled those outside.

No, it means that the same God who scattered us at Babel now unites us on God's own terms—as delightfully diverse and different people who are made one in Christ. The One who told us to scatter at creation now bids us to come together at Pentecost, to a very new sort of community, the church—a people who know no boundaries or distinctions under the towering love of God.

Every Sunday we gather here to relive that story of what

happened at Pentecost. God says, "Come unto me," and we do, so that we might go into all the world and make disciples of all.

Pentecost is a big day for the church because the scattered curse of Babel has become the scattered promise of Pentecost, the promise that God's love leaps over our petty divisions; God's call brings us together.

*   *   *

When scripture is placed next to congregational conflict in a sermon, as was done here, the scripture can function in its native habitat and today's congregations can experience again the same dynamic that is at the heart of the Bible itself. The tower of Babel story in Genesis 11:1-11 arose out of a conflict or question within the faith community. The way the Bible dealt with that conflict can be a guide for us today.

In chapters 1 and 2 we examined the nature of conflict and the pastor as conflict manager in the congregation. The danger of this image of pastoral leadership is that it implies that the minister is simply another professional, a bureaucratic manager of another volunteer organization who, like any other manager, must deal with occasional conflict. While we can learn from the insights of organizational management, and indeed tried to do so in the first two chapters, let us be careful that we do not take the parallels too far.

The pastor is not simply concerned that conflict in the church be managed, he is concerned that it be responded to in a way that is faithful, in a way that is congruent with the demands of the gospel. Being a pastor would be a much easier job if the pastor were merely a manager whose job it was to keep the lid on things at the branch office called St. John's on the Expressway. But a pastor is called to assist in building up the body of Christ, to preach the word of God, and to call people to ever more faithful discipleship. A pastor's response to crisis within the body will therefore be determined by those means and ends which are demanded by the gospel.

Because the pastor who responds to conflict is also the preacher, the pastor's response to crisis will always be in dialogue with the gospel. The pastor is not called simply to do good things for the church but to do Christian things for the church. The preaching task helps us to keep necessary theological focus and content within our management of conflict. Preaching keeps reminding us that "success" in the church's dealing with crisis is not measured by criteria such as what works, what is permissible, the greatest good for the greatest number, he who has most power gets most attention, or other secular criteria. Our response to conflict is, like our preaching, part of the church's attempt to listen to the story of God and to embody that story in our lives.

Because the church is rightly judged by the character of the people who comprise the church, our response to conflict is part of our witness to the world that Jesus Christ makes possible a people who are able to live with one another in hope and peace. Christ has given us the means of living with one another without the fear and violence that constitute human relations in the world.

A great deal depends upon a pastor's image of his or her function. The image of the manager implies an organizational functionary who rather impersonally and nonjudgmentally manages the various units of an organization toward some end product. But the image of the preacher implies that one is able to take a personal stand and to speak with confidence about the truth. Pastoral duties cannot be neatly separated into church administration, homiletics, pastoral care, or theology, as these tasks are so unfortunately separated in seminary curriculum. A pastor is always a preacher, one called to proclaim the gospel in each situation. A preacher is always a pastor, one called to edify the body of Christ in this time and place. Our contention that the sermon is an appropriate place for the pastor to deal with congregational conflict arises out of our confidence that preaching and worship leadership are the central pastoral tasks that give meaning and direction to all other pastoral responsibilities.

What Preaching Cannot Do

Sometimes I think that we preachers hold two extreme views about the importance of preaching. Some of us are surprisingly underinvested in our preaching and others are unrealistically overinvested. Those of us who are underinvested allow any other pastoral activity to crowd out our time for sermon preparation. Pastoral care, that's where the action is, we say—helping people get better. Besides, people have a great deal of faith in the efficacy of counseling and therapy, more faith than they may have in preaching. But laypeople sit there on Sunday in bafflement, wondering why the preacher is so obviously unprepared when he or she had all week to get ready to preach. Or we busy ourselves in the tasks of administration—managing committees, planning and evaluating activities, running the church. If intrachurch conflict is to be managed, one might think of managing it here, in the meeting, rather than there, in the pulpit.

One need not search far to uncover the reasons for our underinvestment in preaching. Preaching is difficult, requiring a diverse collection of skills of biblical interpretation, oral communication, organization, delivery, and intellect. Such skills require time to acquire and time to utilize, and time is not in abundance for pastors. Preaching also requires confidence—confidence in one's own abilities and confidence in the value of the endeavor. In a world of television and slick, professional announcers, can the ordinary preacher compete? When we enter the pulpit, we are required to "put up or shut up," as far as our own values are concerned. We are forced to take a stand, declare publicly where we are, and commit ourselves.

It is easier to spend my time in meetings or filling out reports or visiting the sick than to preach.

There are other pastors who are unrealistically overinvested in preaching. They are convinced that nothing they do as a pastor is as worthwhile as what they do in the pulpit. Pastors tend to downplay sociological factors in favor of theological ones when assessing their congregations. Rather than admit that their church is located in a neighborhood, from which they can expect to draw few new members, the pastor declares that, if the church would just get back to solid biblical preaching or sound theology or energetic evangelism, then everything would change.

They expect great results from preaching and are severely disappointed when preaching doesn't change things. The way they see it, people ought to be able to change if someone tells them they ought to change. This is the intellectualist fallacy—the fallacious belief that the simple inculcation of right ideas automatically produces right behavior and right attitudes. If the gospel is true, as they know it to be, then the truth alone ought to make things happen.

In our better moments we know that this is more magic than ministry. There are too many good reasons—reasons having to do with the nature of the gospel and reasons having to do with human nature—why people don't change simply by being told in sermons, even very good sermons, that they ought to change. If we could change, we would not need Jesus to die for our sin. Human perversity enables us to keep immune from the truth, even when the truth is well spoken.

In this book we will refrain from making exaggerated claims for the efficacy of preaching when applied to congregational conflict. No magic formula is soon to be presented that will enable preaching to be the key to successful resolution of congregational problems. Preaching provides no "quick fix" for conflict, because there is no substitute for committed, patient, long-term pastoral work before and after the pastor stands up to preach. But we will declare that, without preaching, any attempt to minister to intrachurch conflict is in danger of being unfaithful, even if it is "effective," as the world defines success. Preaching may not settle conflict, but it places us within the proper context whereby our conflicts have the possibility of being settled in a way that is faithful to the demands of the gospel. Preaching may not resolve a specific problem, but its word of hope, peace, and judgment enables us to see our lives, and the problem, as an opportunity to experience the gospel in our time and place.

To Speak or Not

Your parishioners grant you, as a pastor, authority and esteem because of your special role in the church. When you speak, they tend to listen not only because of their personal regard for you but also because of their sense that it is your particular responsibility to preach for the church. To fail to understand this is to risk being much more authoritarian than you may mean to be. There are many who will be unable to distinguish between the pastor's words and the word of God. Don't underestimate your own power over the lives of your people; to do so is to be in danger of carelessly using your influence for the wrong ends.

Because you have authority, your words will be magnified in the minds of many of your parishioners. If you truly want to minister to conflict creatively, you don't want your words to drown all other ideas and opinions. You know enough to know that creative resolution may be dependent upon hearing the various options within an issue. After you have spoken from the pulpit, some may bury their own ideas, saying, "He's the preacher and he ought to know what's right." Others may think that you are unfairly attempting totally to control the situation and quietly resent your inserting yourself into the fray. Your words from the pulpit may also intensify the conflict—raise the stakes, so to speak. Before it was a conflict over how to set budget priorities; now it is a matter of whether or not we are going to be faithful to God! Because of the mention of the dispute in a sermon, an organizational conflict has been intensified into a theological battle.

You, the preacher, have spoken, and in so doing you have lost ideas, creative solutions, and future support. You have told the people what ought to be done and now they are quiet, but the calm has been won at great cost.

It is well to respect your pastoral authority, to exercise that authority, whenever possible, to offer open-ended diagnosis of the problem rather than straightforward solutions. In so doing, you give some of your authority to the congregation. If you wanted to, you could perhaps simply declare what ought to be done and order the congregation to do it. But that may be leading your congregation "as the Gentiles" and not in the manner of Christ. Congregational enthusiasm, involvement, and ownership of issues may be lost. If things don't work out, there is no one to blame but the pastor!

In deciding whether or not to speak to an issue, timing is crucial. In general, your ideas ought to be offered late in the discussion of the conflict. You may want to speak early in order to lay down some general ground rules for the ensuing debate: "This congregation faces a tough choice in the months ahead: shall we sell this building and move to the suburbs, or shall we stay and make our stand here? I'm not going to tell you what to decide, because I have not decided myself. This is your church. But I want to say *how* we are going to decide, in a manner that is appropriate for God's people who worship here." Then the preacher discusses the need for mutual respect, love, and consideration as the issue is debated.

The difficulty in the matter of timing is that, if you speak too soon, useful debate may be smothered after your *ex cathedra* pronouncement. On the other hand, if you really do have a strong opinion about the matter under discussion in the congregation, people may think you are deceitful not to express it now. You are not the genius who comes in, after they have spent much painful effort to resolve the conflict, and explains to them what you have known all along. You are the humble servant, servant of the congregation and also of the word of God. You must testify, as humbly and honestly as you can, to what you have heard in serving the congregation and in listening to the word. Of course, you can be humble about it. You, perhaps better than anyone else in the congregation, know the diversity, the complexity, the real human dilemmas behind issues that others may think are simple. They think issues are simple because they see only their side. You, as pastor, are privileged to view the complexity of the issue as you go about your pastoral duties. That knowledge may keep you humble.

To speak or not to speak may be not only a matter of a preacher's assessment of the situation but also a matter of the preacher's self-image. From what I observe, the predominant pastoral psychological stance is passive-aggressive. We appear to be gentle, passive, compliant people on the surface, but underneath we are hostile and angry. We find it difficult to be up front with our disagreements with parishioners. So we swallow our disagreements at the meeting and allow them to ooze out later, in the sermon.

Many of us pastors are honest enough to admit that we would be most uncomfortable in the world of business where hard-nosed decisions must be made and the needs of people must sometimes be subordinated to concern for profit. We like to think of ourselves as engaged in reconciliation rather than in confrontation. Sometimes we fear confrontation because we feel very vulnerable and dependent upon the goodwill of our congregation. You have authority, yes, but much of that authority is sustained through your relationships in the congregation. You do not have power simply because the Bible says so or because the bishop has appointed you. Your power rests on an elaborate and often very fragile network of relationships that may crumble if you abuse your influence. The voluntary nature of the church and the structural dependence of the pastor form a volatile mix that can either deaden human vitality or generate rebirth.

More often, we fear confrontation because we find it difficult to confront the people whom we have learned to love with anything that is unpleasant. Sometimes it is easier to be confrontational in the pulpit than in the one-to-one counseling session—the pulpit offers us some distance and protection. But we are not dealing with strangers. We are not the visiting prophet who is able to blow in, blow off, and then blow out of town. We stand before the people with whom we have been intimate. The visiting expert may expound on the "evils of our materialism," but we know Joe and Mary Jones and their tireless efforts to provide a better life for their children than they had. An outsider may see nothing but sexism within your congregation, but you see real people caught in the conflicting claims and difficult relationships that make relationships between the sexes so problematic.

I preached with vigor against the racist attitudes I heard in my first little church. Later, my sermons became tempered as I really got to know these people. I was still against racism and thought it an offense against the gospel. But I came to admit that many of my racial attitudes had been conditioned by my education, my family, and my experiences—privileges that had been denied most members of my congregation. Many of their attitudes were due to simple ignorance or lack of exposure to others. Their racism was still a sin, but at least it was a more understandable sin and my lack of racism seemed less a virtue than a mere circumstance of fate.

Generally speaking, pastors tend to show more avoidance of conflict in their pulpits, for all the reasons mentioned above, than confrontation in the pulpit.

Some say that we should not speak about conflict from the pulpit when we are unsure of our personal motives for addressing the conflict. In chapter 2 we suggested that it is important for the pastor honestly to ask, Why am I confronting this conflict? Who am I as I insert myself into this situation? What are my real motives here?

But such questions are difficult to answer. As a preacher, you are not speaking objectively, dispassionately, and impersonally on some abstract issue—if you are, you are probably boring people to death! You preach, to a great extent, from your own needs. I remember my surprise at having to admit to myself that I preach because I need to, because I enjoy the act of preaching, because I need the response of others to what I say. It is impossible not to preach from your own needs. Do not sublimate those needs; rather, claim them and even consider sharing them in the sermon. Your acknowledgment of your own self-interest in this conflict may help others to be honest about their self-interest. Your words will be heard with a new sense of trust because of your honesty.

Take the Initiative

We speak to a crisis from the pulpit not simply so that the issue may be "solved" and that we can move on to something important. The crisis is not a roadblock to real ministry but is an occasion for real ministry. If faith is to be vital, it must shed light on the crucial situations of our lives. A congregational crisis is so frightening because the congregation instinctively senses that, if its Christian faith cannot be of help here, it cannot be of help anywhere. Will all of our fellowship, worship, service, and witness provide guidance in this situation, or will we be left to our own devices?

In the latter part of the twentieth century, we find ourselves at the end of a process that began after the Middle Ages—the slow erosion of Christian claims as a key to every aspect of life. It isn't that we are less religious than our forebears, it's just that we are overwhelmed by a cafeteria of "religions," all promising to make sense out of life. Added to this theological competition is the nomadic existence of our lives in which we are forced to leave behind friends, family, and teachers and to re-create community amidst strangers. Values become chosen on the basis of our personal desires rather than communally bestowed.

In defense against this fearful situation, many simply withdraw from the search for truth. They resist making any emotional investment, they cease to care. Having lost faith in the value of faith, they no longer look to the church for help in the quest for meaning.

If the church is to survive in this marketplace of meaning, it must show that it is capable of overcoming our fear and confronting the tough issues of life. Christianity promises freedom, not freedom from struggle and pain but freedom from fear. Fear is to be overcome not by avoidance but by refusal to evade its presence, by our naming the name of the One who claims to have "overcome the world." Every time we boldly confront crisis and conflict in the family of God, we witness to the truth that Jesus really does make possible a community based on hope and trust. Every time we choose to evade the crisis and keep silent, we imply that our faith is not strong enough to enable us to have courage in crisis.

Pastors cannot rely on the laity to begin the task of calling attention to a congregational crisis. In rare situations, usually after the laity have reached the point of utter frustration and exasperation, laypersons may take the initiative, but often they do so in ways that only accentuate factionalism and fragmentation. It is the pastor's job to open up these questions. The pastor bears the tough community-bestowed burden of placing the gospel alongside the crisis. While pastors are not the only source of spiritual power within the congregation, they are the designated leaders who provide a model of how to overcome fear of failure and destruction and to trust God to help preserve the church that God wants. This usually means that the pastor must persistently introduce creative tension into the congregation in order that the congregation may have the frightening but utterly essential opportunity of experiencing itself as being faithful.

Sometimes the pastor must be prepared to go it alone. It is of the nature of any human group to try to protect the status quo and avoid confronting the discomfort that people feel. But pastors cannot surrender their responsibility to see that the process of reflection begins—both for the good of themselves and for the parish as a whole. Ultimate resolution of the crisis will rarely occur in listening to a sermon.

More than likely, the conflict will be resolved only after long and sometimes painful negotiation, discussion, and compromise. But the first step is to break the ice. Doing so requires a considerable amount of pastoral integrity and confidence. In speaking, pastors expose themselves to the weapons of any voluntary association—criticism, withdrawal, or the neutralizing of the power of the leader. No wonder many pastors simply avoid the confrontation and preach on more acceptable subjects. The conflict may be avoided, but the price may be the very purpose and vitality of the church, the denial of a marvelous opportunity to witness to the power of the Christian faith.

4

The Pastor Who Is Prophet

Many have documented the sad consequences of the early days of the pastoral care movement in which pastoral care moved from essential biblical, theological, and liturgical foundations to the social sciences. Much was gained from the insights of psychology and sociology when applied to the life of the church. Indeed, this book is heavily dependent upon the work of secular thought in the area of conflict management and the behavior of individuals and groups in crisis. But eventually any insights gleaned from the social sciences must bow to the theological commitments of the church if the church is to continue as church. The pastoral ministry is much more than simply doing "good" things for people. Our theology defines for us what is good, what to value, what to work for and look for in our congregational life.

As Paul says, "From now on, therefore, we regard no one from a human point of view" (2 Cor. 5:16). The pastor offers more than healing and sustaining ministry. The pastor must also offer guidance, remembering that pastoral assertiveness is also a means of caring. For too long pastoral care, using the model of psychology, shied away from the idea that the pastor's judgment had any part in the helping process. But pastoral indifference can be as destructive as the pastor's overbearing judgments. The history of pastoral care in the United States shows the tendency of pastors to adopt the prevalent self-culture of American society with its emphasis on adjustment, self-realization, and the radical personalization of the gospel. The pastor cares, not for isolated individuals, but for the family of God and its health.

The one who preaches is more than an administrator of a voluntary organization who occasionally must confront a crisis in that organization. The one who preaches is more than a conflict manager. In the last couple of chapters we have noted that the one who preaches is also a pastor, one who is intimately involved in the lives of those who are members of the congregation. Now we link another biblical image to our portrait of the one who preaches—the prophet. The pastor who cares for the congregation is also the prophet who must speak God's word to the household of God.

The Prophet

Walter Brueggemann says, "The task of prophetic ministry is to nurture, nourish, and evoke a consciousness and perception alternative to the consciousness and perception of the dominant culture around us."[8] God's prophet deliberately evokes in situations a newness that confronts decadent systems of belief and practice. The prophet is more than the "angry young man" or the carping social critic whose alienation from the culture is mirrored in his or her shrill denouncements of society. The prophet, in Brueggemann's opinion, is the poet, the artist who contends with false fields of perception, idolatrous value systems, and arrogant rulers by articulating an imaginative, evocative vision for the faith community.

Most cultural systems deprecate history, make idols of the "now," enthrone the present as the only possible arrangement, and ridicule hope. In such situations, our memory becomes a subversive resource for transforming the present. So many of the biblical prophet's words were words of memory and recollection. The prophet is not so much about the business of addressing public crises that arise from time to time but rather confronting the underlying root causes and the myopic vision that leads to injustice. The prophet's words will be words of criticism and confrontation, dismantling and breaking down, so that envisioning and dreaming, reconstruction and revolution might occur.

In words and images, the prophet hopes to evoke in the people an alternative mind-set that arises out of God's promises for us. Brueggemann notes that, in the exodus, Israel emerges as the alternative culture, the alternative consciousness to that of Egypt. The oppression of the Egyptian royal system is confronted by the compassion and justice of God as articulated by Moses. In the resultant struggle, there is confrontation, dismantling, and delegitimatizing. Egypt's gods are exposed as silly idols.

Brueggemann says that prophetic preaching begins with criticism. The criticism emerges first out of grief—the recognition that things are not right. Grief is not resignation; rather, it is a powerful act of criticism, of making public our hurt. These public cries demand answers.

Then comes the alternative, energizing promise of hope and newness. New realities are seen that could not have been seen without the prophetic imagination. There is struggle and unknowing, risk and uncertainty, even as there was struggle and fear during the exodus. But the prophet calls people to trust that God really is involved in their life together, bringing the people to something better and more faithful.

A Case in Point

In the congregation, the pastor doesn't simply react to crises when they arise. The pastor is also the prophet who evokes a vision in the congregation of what it means to be God's people. That vision produces crises, and if the vision is compelling, the crises may produce growth. What follows is an example of how one pastor led his congregation into unexplored territory.[9] I offer it here because it depicts, in a concrete way, the interplay between the pastoral, prophetic, and priestly roles of the minister and because it shows us some of the many factors that affect our preaching with the congregation.

> Broadway United Methodist Church in South Bend, Indiana, is in one of those sections of town that began to decline about 20 years ago but did not quite hit bottom. In the early '60s, when a highway was cut through a mainly black area of the city, poor, mostly black, people began to rent in the neighborhood. The neighborhood is integrated, and many young couples have begun moving back into the area, since it provides reasonably priced housing.

The church has a large building, witnessing to its once large and lively congregation. The congregation now numbers about 100 members, with Sunday attendance averaging between 40 and 60. The integration of the church in the early '60s, coupled with a series of unsuccessful pastorates, nearly sealed the church's doom. Denominational executives felt there was little chance of recovery.

However, in the early '70s a pastor was appointed to Broadway who refused to believe the church was doomed. What others saw as a problem, he saw as an exciting possibility. By visiting the sick, preaching, organizing the church, and developing an urban ministry, the pastor imbued the members of the congregation with a new sense of confidence in their value to one another and, in particular, to the neighborhood. The members became determined to do much more than survive.

About five years ago, a board meeting took place at the church. The first agenda item concerned the leaky roof over the education building. Since the church no longer had an active Sunday school, the building was used primarily by the church's Headstart program. The necessary repairs would cost at least $5,000—a huge sum for the church. After much discussion, the board voted to accept the most expensive bid because that kind of roof would last the longest.

What was remarkable about this decision was what was not discussed. No one suggested that the church ought to rethink its investment in the neighborhood. No one suggested relocating in the suburbs. No one even noticed that the church, by its decision, was saying that it would rather be a presence in this neighborhood than a success elsewhere.

But the neighborhood noticed. The machinery that pulled up to the church to do the reroofing was a sign to the neighbors that they were not to be abandoned, at least not by this church. Of course, some might suggest that the church ought to have spent money on the emergency food pantry instead. But that was not a real choice, since the building had to be maintained first if the congregation were to show its commitment to being God's people on the southeast side of town.

The next item on the agenda seemed to have more significant ecclesiological implications. The worship committee had suggested celebrating the Eucharist every Sunday. Because of its evangelical background, the church had a tradition of celebrating the Eucharist infrequently. The new pastor, however, had gradually increased the frequency until the church was now celebrating the Eucharist almost 30 times a year. The congregation had responded favorably to this practice.

This positive attitude toward the Eucharist was due in great part to the patient work of the pastor. He had always been candid about his desire to have an every-Sunday Eucharist, but he never forced his will on the congregation. Through his preaching, by taking the Eucharist to many members in nursing homes and those too ill to come to church, and in countless other ways, he had helped people see how the Eucharist made caring for one another intelligible. His sermons were evocative attempts to help the congregation see what the church could be. For a congregation trapped in wistful memories of what the church had been and terrified by what their church appeared to be today, this sermonic envisioning was crucial. Here was a preacher who had a definite idea of where the church ought to be going and didn't mind saying so. But here also was a preacher who didn't mind taking the time to be patient and wait for this congregation to hear and to embody his vision.

Some undoubtedly put up with the pastor's "high-church views" because they loved and respected him; but they also were learning that this type of pastoral care was determined by the Eucharist.

As the board prepared to vote on the proposal, it was shocked to hear the pastor, who tended to say little at meetings, announce, "You should not vote on this." The pastor seemed to have lost all political sense. A matter for which he had worked for years was coming to a vote, which he would win, and he would not let it happen.

He explained that though it is the tradition of the church that the Eucharist be served every Sunday, the congregation no more had the right to decide how often the Eucharist would be celebrated than to decide whether it would say the Lord's Prayer. Both were obligations it was invited to obey or, rather, they were privileges in which the church ought to rejoice.

He then suggested that he would announce to the church that there was strong sentiment in favor of having the Eucharist every Sunday, but recognizing that there might be some who strongly dissented from this policy, he would announce a time for people to express their disagreement. If many felt strongly that such a move would make it impossible for them to continue to worship there, then, he said, the church might have to wait a little longer. Not to wait, he suggested, would belie the very unity of the Eucharist. The board agreed. Two meetings to air views on this subject were called. Since no one came to either, the church simply began having the Eucharist every Sunday.

Though it is generally assumed that Protestant churches that favor "high-church stuff" are affluent churches that are more aesthetically than socially aware, such was not the case at Broadway. About three months after the board meeting, the outreach committee came to the church with a proposal. Unemployment had hit the city hard, and soup kitchens had sprung up to feed the city's poor. But the committee felt that a soup kitchen, as much good as it might do, was not what the church needed to provide. Instead, the committee suggested that since the church had learned the significance of sharing the eucharistic meal together, perhaps it could share a meal with the neighborhood. Such a meal would not be the same as the Eucharist, but at least it would express the kind of community that that meal made possible. The proposal was that every Sunday at worship people be invited to come to lunch.

The proposal was approved, and the church was divided into five groups, each taking responsibility to prepare a meal for one Sunday. Often between 40 and 60 people appeared for the Sunday lunch. A few who shared the meal might come to church before the lunch, but the church gained no new members from the effort. The meal made it clear that the church was not simply another social agency doing a little good, but a people called to witness God's presence in the world. The presence that comes in the meal sustained the church's ability to be present in the neighborhood, a symbol that all was not lost.

Because it is the nature of any human group to protect the status quo, there is in most congregations an unspoken wish to avoid confronting potentially controversial issues such as those faced by Broadway Church. The designation of some-one as a "prophet" is therefore synonymous with rejection. When confronted with a crisis within the congregation, pastors may resolve it in at least four ways, the majority of which are ultimately detrimental. First, they may tune out, focusing their sermons on nicer thoughts, or they may actively abuse the congregation's system of belief. Abuse may take the form of sermons that say, in effect, "You people are too conservative and old-fashioned. God wants us to change and to move into new areas of service. This church is too traditional to be a real church." If organizational changes are needed, the preacher will ridicule the church for being out of touch with proper denominational organization schemes. If some modification in the style of worship is being advocated, the preacher will marvel, "You mean to tell me that no one here has seen the new hymnal! I can't believe you are so behind the times."

When pastors tune out or abuse the congregational value system, they forfeit their adoption by the congregation as persons of trust whose authority is increasingly respected. Failing to be adopted by the congregation, they fail to gain power to lead. The lay leadership will either seek to oust them through open conflict or may lapse into apathy or avoidance.

A second alternative is for the pastor to adopt the parish's value system in entirety and forfeit the ability to introduce creative tension into the life of the parish. The preacher who says, "I am more of a pastor, ministering to the needs of people, than a prophet who is always trying to stir up trouble" is often the preacher who cares more about self-protection than the needs of people. A primary need of the congregation is for enough tension between its present life and the life that the gospel demands, to keep things alive and challenging.

A third way is for the pastors passively to refuse to address any of the real issues involved in conflict as genuine differences between themselves and the laity if they emerge. They thus abandon the congregation to a life of discord (as laypersons compete for leadership in order to fill the leadership vacuum made by an incompetent pastor) and spiritual lethargy.

The example of Broadway Church reminds us that pastors cannot rely on the laity to take the initiative in confronting the pain of unmet expectations and conflicting values within the congregation. In contrast to the three options above, the pastor at Broadway knew that pastors have a responsibility to see that reflection begins by resisting the pressures of both apathy and fear within themselves and others. The pulpit can be the place where the roles of pastor and prophet mesh in the role of preacher. How different would the story of Broadway be if their pastor had not been a prophet.

Broadway also reminds us that a parish exists in an environment over which it has some influence and which has some influence upon it. For Broadway, it was decaying inner-city South Bend. Generally speaking, the external environment has much more power over a congregation than the congregation likes to admit. The congregation is one interactive part of a larger social system. When there is conflict or radical change within the surrounding community, the congregation must react in order to remain viable. But these facts would be true whether we were speaking of a church or an auto repair shop.

A church is different from many other organizations in that it is a voluntary organization. Any person in the church is free not to participate in its life and work. Sometimes laypersons exercise this prerogative and withdraw their participation, financial support, or membership in the face of controversy. No congregation can be any stronger in dealing with conflict than the commitment of its members to struggle to be faithful. Broadway Church had begun, like most churches begin and remain, as a group that was formed on the basis of sociological factors related to income, education, class, race, family background, and social aspirations rather than theological factors per se. Where we live is a greater influence on most congregations than what we believe.

But now Broadway Church had become a group that perceived itself as more united in its commitment to follow Jesus Christ than in sociological homogeneity. The members were consciously aware of themselves as being different from their neighbors. Broadway's pastor undoubtedly expended more effort helping members react to, witness before, and resist the surrounding community than helping them to adjust to their sociological setting. The homiletical response to congregational crises will thus be influenced by the surrounding community and the congregation's perception of itself and the community.

The example of Broadway Church also illustrates that a congregation is a collaborative venture between clergy and laity. Communication between both is essential if the church is to develop its capacities to handle crisis. In American churches, the clergy tend to be more committed than the laity to involvement of the church in controversial issues. However, the clergy may have more reasons to be threatened by conflict within the congregation.

Conflict becomes most deadly when the parties to the

conflict stop talking to one another. Preaching is part of the total communicative process between pastor and people. Of course, the pastor is not only the person who appears each Sunday morning to deliver a word from on high. All week the pastor has been involved in the give-and-take of Bible study groups, board meetings, informal encounters, and hospital visitations. These opportunities for communication are an essential prelude and follow-up to the task of communicating from the pulpit. But the sermon becomes an important occasion for the pastor to declare his or her vision for the congregation. The laypeople are listening for that vision and appreciate the preacher's forthright attempts to state what he or she feels is the future direction for the church. The congregation at Broadway knew that the pastor had commitments to every-Sunday Eucharist. Fortunately the pastor had the ability to articulate this commitment without forcing it down anyone's throat, and his forthright statement of intentions helped to build a climate of trust. He had laid his cards on the table.

Note that in the discussion of the life at Broadway, there is an inevitable distancing of pastor from the congregation. Every time the pastor stands in the pulpit and preaches, there is a gap that separates pastor from people. Some preachers resist this separation, longing to come out of the pulpit and sit in the pew. But the example of Broadway illustrates how important the maintenance of distance is for the vitality of the congregation. The gospel itself sets up a distance between the prophet who bears the word and the people who hear it. Of course, the one who bears the word must also have heard the word. But the gospel is about the gap between where we are and where God would have us be. It can be a lonely enterprise to speak that word.

Luther spoke of the gospel as the "external word." Many are weary of self-centeredness, a self-centeredness that is too often confirmed in our self-help, psychologically oriented sermons. The pastor at Broadway began by respecting the integrity and identity of the congregation as he found it. But he did not stop there. He brought the people a word, a vision that could not have come to them had he not spoken.

It requires courage to break the ice and speak to a congregational dilemma. A high degree of personal autonomy enables a pastor to risk exposing himself or herself to the ultimate weapon of a voluntary association—the power to criticize, withdraw support, or neutralize the authority of the leader.

Preachers should not be surprised that they feel lonely, isolated in the midst of a crisis. There are functional and theological reasons for this isolation. The clergy is the only professional group in our society dependent upon the group it serves for both its income and its supervision. Rewards are determined almost wholly by others. Given this reality, the temptation of the preacher is often to capitulate to the lowest common denominator of expectation within the congregation or to lash out in anger against those who are being served. The soothing honey-voiced and insipid "pastoral" preacher or the abrasive critical "prophetic" preacher, who seem so different, are often the result of the same reality.

In contrast to these unhealthy responses to the isolation of the preacher is the way of leadership that builds a constituency. The first step toward building a constituency lies, as it did at Broadway, in the preacher self-consciously choosing a faith stance and articulating the consequences of that stance. Good preachers are those who work at first uncovering their own commitments, expressing them to themselves before they attempt to communicate them to others. If the preacher conceives of himself or herself as little more than one who stands up on Sunday morning and tries to express the present consensus of the congregation at that moment, then the congregation can expect little leadership, or even few interesting sermons, from the pulpit. While there is a time for the preacher to listen, now we are talking about the need for the preacher to speak. Unless the humility of the good listener is compounded with the boldness of the good speaker, preaching will be of little value to the life of the church.

Then the preacher is able to build a constituency around his or her commitments. This will require negotiation. "You said today in your sermon that . . . ," says one parishioner, "but I don't feel that this answer is adequate." Now the stage is set for dialogue to occur. The first step is in the communication of a dream: "Thy kingdom come, thy will be done, on earth as it is in heaven" (Matt. 6:10). The pastor at Broadway had a vision, perhaps not clear at first but taking form in his first months of ministry there, of what this church could be. To a dispirited and despondent congregation, he communicated this vision, not only in the pulpit but certainly there, of what Broadway was and could be. Then he engaged in the long, patient, time-consuming task of negotiation.

Because churches are voluntary religious associations, their stability depends in equal parts upon a consensus about the vision and the purposes of the congregation and upon the satisfaction that the members receive from their participation. The consensus that is needed is not simple agreement for decision-making but is much more organic. There is an intricate network of meanings within the congregation that supply direction for the people. Consensus refers to an agreed-upon set of perceptions and norms that give identity to a particular church. The pastor at Broadway was explicit about his dreams for the church, yet he was willing to take time and to be patient and wait for the seeds he had planted to take root. He undoubtedly spent many hours listening to the story of Broadway, the history of how it had arrived at this point in time. He waited until he had become part of that history before he tried to make history there. If he had not, he might have been able to swing a few key people to his point of view earlier. But the chances are that his victories would be short-lived. Rather than ascribe some sort of magical powers to his preaching or his pastoral leadership, he let the people have as much time as they needed, to say no, if they must, to his dreams for them. He never forgot that, for better or for worse, Broadway was their church.

This aspect of preaching to congregational conflict is one of the most difficult. I am not a patient person by inclination. As a preacher, I tend to expect preaching to yield almost magical, instantaneous results. If I can simply speak well about what ought to be done, the congregation will do what ought to be done. In my better moments I know this is false. A volunteer group demands time. The pastor at Broadway showed amazing, but wise, restraint. Everyone knew how much he wanted to see his vision become a reality. But everyone also knew that he had enough respect for the integrity of the congregation to wait until his words took form in the life of the people. Rather than frame the problem in terms of power, the pastor at Broadway chose to frame it in terms of information, education, consensus, and understanding. This way takes longer, but in the end it yields more long-term results.

The Pastor

Pastoral patience arises out of trust in the word. Even as the sower must trust the seed to take root, so we must trust the word to accomplish, in its own time, what the word would do. We can't make the people listen. We hope to remove some of the obstacles, and we hope they are able to hear their word in our words. As Fred Craddock has said, "The Bread of Life is broken and offered, but the hearers must be allowed to chew for themselves."[10]

The preacher at Broadway Church respected the congregation's resistance to the message. Resistance may take many forms, such as decreased attendance, petty criticism, apathy, or attempts to deflect the discussion to peripheral issues. Jesus preached away more people than he won. Good preaching elicits strong resistance because listeners realize that the preacher is trying to change us and we wonder if the change will be painful. What will we look like after the operation?

Another reason for patience (and some humility) on the part of the prophet is an acknowledgment of the provisional nature of our preaching. Without taking back anything we have said, let us admit that people deserve room to change and grow at their own pace. Sometimes the seeds that the sower plants grow secretly. Other people may reap where we sow and the harvest is God's, not ours. Preaching is our laborious attempt to discern God's word in this time and place. We should allow the congregation to see how we have struggled over an issue, because the people will sense that the struggle implies that there is no simple, easily discernible answer written in the sky. Because the preacher's words have so often been corrected, expanded, or enlivened by the words and lives of his or her parishioners, the preacher more often conceives preaching as dialogue rather than monologue.

What the preacher says will be affected by the perspective

of one who has formed a variety of pastoral relationships with the listeners. What the listeners hear will be affected by the ways in which their lives have been touched by the pastor. A pastor is not a prophet who has gone soft, nor is a prophet a pastor who has lost the ability to care. God is able to "roar from Zion" (Amos 1:2) like a lion and also "feed his flock like a shepherd" and "gather the lambs in his arms" (Isa. 40:11).

The pastor bears the unenviable burden of having to pay attention to all aspects of the congregation at the same time. A congregation is a total system, a living, breathing organism that is constantly being impacted by the personal crises of the members, the changes within the surrounding cultural setting, movements within the denomination as a whole, as well as the theological claims of scripture. To be a pastor is to juggle five or six balls at once, trying to keep them all in the air. That is why, in this book, pronouncements on "Six Steps in Speaking to a Crisis Within the Congregation" or neat examples of "How to Do It Right" are not offered. Preaching is only one part of total pastoral responsibilities. If preaching is done as an isolated act, the congregation will "come unglued."

Our familiar distinctions between the stereotypical "pastor" and "prophet" do not work when we look at concrete examples of churches such as Broadway. We see that a church must have the resources beyond survival if it is to be bold in its ministry. The roof would have to be repaired, the bills would have to be paid, or there would be no social outreach. A solid system of social support must be provided—fellowship—in order to uphold individual members as they struggle to live out their faith commitments. Fortunately, few pastors think to themselves, Now, I am entering the pulpit, where I shall be a prophet. Lines between ministerial functions become delightfully blurred in the actual day-to-day work of the pastor. Whenever "prophetic" action toward the wider community replaces the primary pastoral work of the church in evangelizing and nurturing persons in Christian discipleship, the congregation will not survive. Ministry suffers when the pastor's work becomes compartmentalized, when pastoral care becomes an activity of mainly psychological importance without theological commitments or when preaching is conceived of as talking

about God without taking account of the human consequences of our God talk.

The sermon is much like the prayer of a congregation,
and the prophet who speaks that word is the priest who
leads the congregation in prayer. The prophetic word
comes from outside the congregation, as an extended word,
addressed to the people in their situation. But the sermon
is also the pastoral word that speaks to God for the people.
Earlier we spoke of how the preacher not only speaks to the
people but also speaks for the people. The word is God's,
but it is also the church's word. The word did not arrive in
South Bend the day the new pastor came to town. That
word belonged to Broadway Church. It was inarticulate, an
incoherent groan perhaps, but it was there as surely as
hope, faith, and love were there. The pastor listened to the
people so that he might pray with them. "Teach us to pray,"
the disciples asked Jesus. Preach for us, we do not know how
to speak as we ought, the people at Broadway said to their
pastor.

The preacher is the prophet who speaks God's word to
the congregation in the middle of crisis. But the same
preacher is the pastor who speaks for God's people, giving
voice to the congregation's word in the crisis. When this
happens, the people sit up and listen because the voice they
hear is their own. The sermon is not the minister's profes-
sion, a word delivered from on high to the lowly laity. The
word from God which is *our* word is often the most "prophetic."

Recall Luke's account of the young prophet Jesus before
his hometown synagogue in Nazareth (Luke 4:16–30). Jesus
read them their own, beloved, familiar scriptures. He read
them Isaiah 61, a most familiar passage; then he told them
two familiar stories, about Elijah and Elisha. By their own
tradition, their own scripture, he shocked them into an
awareness that cut so deep it angered them. To hear a word,
in our own dialect, a word that gives voice to our own
inarticulate groans and fears, is really to hear. We can easily
dismiss the visiting prophet from out of town. But to hear
the voice of our pastor—one who knows us, lives with us,
and speaks our language—is to be heard and therefore to
hear in a way that is truly prophetic.

It is the pastor's voice telling a story that enables a con

gregation like Broadway to tell its story in a Christian way, that is, to tell it in a way that gives theological significance to the common things (like putting on a new roof or changing the style of worship) that constitute a church's life. I believe that a major problem with contemporary church life is that we lack the resources to make sense out of the common things we do as Christians—such as praying, baptizing, sharing food, or arguing about a new roof. Lacking the ability to describe theologically the significance of these activities, we resort to sociological, psychological, or managerial descriptions and explanations that lead us to miss the miracle that God is really in our midst.

When it comes down to it, that's all a good preacher wants to do in prophetically preaching the word or pastorally visiting the sick—to refer us to the presence of God. When we preachers forsake our roles and become mere bureaucratic managers of the congregation, we cheat our people of the invigorating opportunity to see that God is closer to us than we once thought.

The preacher who is pastor and prophet is the leader in God's process of forming a visible people who have listened to a different story from that of the world and now struggle in their congregational life to embody that word in their life together.

Bill decided to speak to the issue of accessibility for the handicapped at his church. Like the pastor at Broadway, he laid groundwork. His sermon seemed appropriate. Joe and Janet had other ideas. Here is what happened after the sermon:

Our church is a fellowship of just over three hundred members who worship in a structure built in 1832—a building of classic Connecticut Western Reserve architecture, a well-maintained registered historic building, and a building, alas, not accessible to the handicapped. Into my third year as their pastor, I helped organize a successful capital repairs drive that would enable major renovation work at the church and was to be completed in time to coincide with the church's 150th anniversary. In the light of over $5,000 left over from the drive and the continued inaccessibility to the sanctuary for the handicapped, I began to envision a new drive to provide access for all. Armed with denominational support materials and sketches by several architects,

I lifted the idea before the session and the trustees and then preached a sermon in story form, "Making Way for the Touch of Christ." It dealt with the Lukan text about Jesus healing a paralytic man who had been lowered from a roof by several men into his presence.

Following the service, I was approached by a couple in the church: Joe, a former trustee and a hard-nosed, self-made, businesslike millionaire, and Janet, a leader, heavily involved in presbytery work and very mission-minded. They were influential members, highly regarded, and very generous givers. They had just opened up their home to Janet's ninety-year-old mother, who was crippled. I thought they would be receptive perhaps to chairing a new drive, and I greeted them cordially. However, they were terse and rather cold in their conversation.

JANET: Bill, that was a good sermon and all, and I know you feel good about your idea, but I just can't see it.

BILL: See what, Janet?

JANET: I just can't see us starting a new drive for a ramp . . . or an elevator . . . or whatever.

BILL: Uh-huh.

JANET: It won't work. It's just not practical. It'll cost too much. And—well, who's going to use it? Do we have anyone in this little village who needs it?

BILL: Well, there's Heidi [a three-year-old], and Elsie [a blind ninety-three-year-old in a wheelchair], and Bill [a Vietnam vet paraplegic who teaches at the high school], and—

JOE: Look, Bill, you know me. I'm a businessman. And I gotta always justify costs in terms of return. It just isn't good business sense to spend ten to fifteen grand on some system . . . for maybe three people.

BILL: But how, even if three people—

JOE: Oh, no, Bill. Don't try pulling that on me. It's economically foolish, pure and simple! Kids would play on it . . . some might get hurt. Who'd monitor it? And besides, it'll wreck the building's looks.

JANET: Bill, we've talked it over. Even Mom agrees. We

can't support the project. We won't give any
money.

At first Bill was a bit intimidated by Janet and Joe—which
was probably their intended effect. Joe implies that Bill is a
naive and unrealistic preacher who knows little about the
cold logic of finance; Janet will have none of Bill's impracti-
cality. When Bill attempts to remind them of all the handicapped persons in the congregation, Joe tries to put Bill
down with a remark about justifying costs in terms of return. The preacher must have really upset them to force Joe
and Janet to resort to intimidating tactics and to refuse to
face certain facts.

Bill would be justified in suspecting that, for Joe and
Janet, the wheelchair ramp was a symbol that evoked
strong, though subconscious feelings. For one thing, there
was an argument here about the purpose and meaning of
the church. Is the church a symbol of nostalgia, a society for
the preservation of historic architecture? Or is the church
a place of outreach and compassion? Why had the congregation raised the money for the building renovation? The
pastor might have thought that the renovation was an ex-
tension of the mission of the church. But perhaps the members saw the renovation as an act of nostalgia, as
preservation of the past.

Because he was Joe and Janet's pastor, Bill knew that Joe
and Janet had recently moved her ninety-year-old mother to
their home. Was her presence there, and the life-style
changes that had been required of them since her arrival,
related to their opposition to the ramp? Perhaps the church
was where they came to escape the handicapped rather than
to confront them. They already had too much accessibility!
Their rather heated and direct response to Bill's sermon
could have arisen out of their own struggle at home to
accommodate a handicapped person into their lives. They
heard the sermon. It provoked a crisis in them, a crisis of
recognition, guilt, anger—a host of emotions. In the interplay of his roles as pastor and prophet, Bill had opened the
door for a confrontation between two of his members, himself, and God's word. The prophetic sermon did not end
when Bill stepped from the pulpit—it began!

5

How Shall I Preach?

How we preach is determined by our images of preaching.
How do we view ourselves when we step into the pulpit? As
we speak to some congregational crisis, who are we? Usually
our models of ourselves as preachers are only vaguely
defined in our minds. But even in our unconscious, our
images of ourselves exercise a powerful influence upon
what we say in a sermon and how we choose to say it.
Thomas Sieg has delineated three models of preaching that
are helpful in sorting out our own expectations for preaching.[11]

Three Models of Preaching

The Prophetic Model. In chapter 4 we discussed the image
of the prophet. We noted the complexity of this image and
the helpful control of the prophetic model by our pastoral
work. In the prophetic model the ministry of preaching is
that of the preacher as one specially chosen from the community and gifted by God to give the people a word that
God wants them to hear. "To whom I send you you shall
go, and whatever I command you you shall speak" (Jer. 1:7).
New Testament images of the evangelist sometimes express
a similar theme (2 Tim. 4:1–4).

The two great dimensions of the prophetic model are that
the preacher is specifically called by God for the task of
preaching and that the preacher has insight or knowledge
that is not available to others in the community. The
prophet is set apart. Whether the prophet's special insight

is seen as coming from the inspiration of the Holy Spirit, from the act of ordination, or from superior seminary training, the prophet is clearly seen as one who has a special word for the church. This point of view has significant pastoral implications for how a sermon is prepared and delivered.

Typically, the prophet prepares by relying upon his or her own gifts and insights. Prayer, study, and meditation are carried out in the preacher's study. The prophet is concerned about the community that is to be addressed, but that concern, which reflects the prophet's listening to the congregation, is that the preached word might effectively nourish, heal, and inspire the people. The prophet is somewhat like the physician who approaches a patient or the professor who approaches a lecture hall full of students. The preacher wants to give them something, something they would not have if the preacher had not spoken.

In 1964, David M. Currie was serving the First Presbyterian Church of Durham. One year before, the city had been on the verge of martial law when blacks attempted to integrate many city facilities. On May 3, 1964, a young black man came forward in response to the minister's regular invitation to persons to join the congregation and asked to join First Presbyterian. Currie says of that day, "By evening rumors and garbled information abounded. By midweek it was judged wise to send to the congregation a letter stating what had happened at the session meeting the previous Sunday. The letter included a citation of Matthew 16:13–26 as the text for next Sunday's sermon. Members were requested to read and pray over this text, and to come to worship the next Sunday."[12] After having laid the groundwork in the letter the previous week, Currie preached a sermon on Matthew 16:13–26 which began:

> Profound actions and reactions have stirred within the life of this congregation during the last seven days. It is incumbent upon disciples of Jesus that these actions and reactions be seen in the light of the will and Word of Jesus Christ who alone is head of the church. To that end I have asked you, through a letter last week, to read and pray over the text, Matthew 16:13–26.
>
> Three points of emphasis will be drawn from this text today: (1) The church is Jesus'—he is its builder and Lord; (2)

persons upon whom and through whom Jesus builds the
church are fallible; and (3) discipleship within the church is
costly—but richly rewarding.[13]

Currie went on to develop these three points. He moved
from theological affirmations about the nature of Christ's
relationship to the church to specific applications related to
our discipleship. In so doing, he spoke as one who came
with a word for the people, a word addressed to them from
a prophet.

The Representative Model. The representative preacher
puts great stress upon knowing and identifying with the
people to whom he or she is speaking. This does not mean
that the preacher is elected by the congregation, although
that may have happened. It means that the representative
is both the listener and the speaker to the community. Like
the prophet, the representative feels called for the specific
task of preaching. But unlike the prophet, the representative does not see himself or herself as the only member of
the community gifted with insights or knowledge to be
shared with the others. The gifts of the Spirit are distributed
among many in the congregation. The representative seeks
to discern the moving of the Spirit within the community.
Often, in the midst of conflict within the congregation, the
representative preacher will direct the congregation's attention to the presence of God within this crisis and suggest
ways to respond to that presence.

Listening is particularly important for the representative
preacher. The representative is prepared to receive insights
from the congregation, as people struggle with the demands of discipleship. The preacher will also listen to biblical scholars and others who have dedicated their lives to
careful listening to scripture. After having listened, the
preacher draws on all that has been seen and heard and
makes use of it in the preaching moment. The representative preacher aims at inviting the whole community into the
task of preparing and delivering sermons, always hoping
that the particular congregation will recognize itself in the
sermon. Whereas the prophet might think of himself or
herself as a speaker, the representative sees himself or herself in dialogue.

This doesn't mean that the sermon takes the form of a

dialogue, although one could see that some sermons could, particularly those which try to be fair to two opposing ideas within the congregation. The sermon could be written for two speakers, thesis and antithesis, who represent, in what they say, two viewpoints. In listening to the sermon, the congregation might come to a new synthesis on the issue at hand.

Sermon discussion groups might also be helpful to the representative preacher. A regular program of pastoral visitation, and other ways of intentionally listening to the word of the congregation before delivering a word from the pulpit, will be seen by the representative preacher as essential preparation. We shall discuss dialogue and feedback opportunities in the next section.

In pastoral counseling, the preacher develops skills that may be transferred into the task of representative preaching. Howard Clinebell describes the steps in a typical counseling situation: (1) Help the person examine and explore alternative approaches to the problem. What is the problem and how might it be addressed? (2) After alternatives have been explored, move toward making a choice of the most promising alternative and take concrete steps toward implementing the choice. (3) Offer guidance in the form of ideas, information, and tentative suggestions. At this point the therapist provides a conceptual map of the choices that are beginning to take shape. This conceptualizing aids the person to begin to take charge, to "own" the situation and decide, "This is what I am now going to do."[14]

Whereas the prophetic preacher brings something to the situation, the representative preacher finds something to bring out of the situation. The prophet primarily proclaims; the representative evokes. Like the prophet, the representative wants to effect a change in the listeners. The representative ought to be honest about his or her desire to work change. Yet the representative sees change as the result of considerable self-exploration. Pushing too soon for a decision will be counterproductive. The representative preacher knows that preaching is not an impersonal process. All the preacher's personal relationships with the listeners are brought to bear in the act of preaching. As they listen, members of the congregation want the preacher to succeed. They want the preacher to be able to be clear and persuasive. Resistance will occur and the preacher's constant attentiveness to the mood, the spoken and unspoken attitudes of the congregation, will help to uncover such resistance. The resistance to change may not be easily overcome, but at least the representative preacher will be better able to know the conditions whereby the resistance may be reduced because of his or her relationships in the congregation.

There is a danger that representative sermons can become simply an ambivalent voicing: "On the one hand . . . but on the other hand." But the strength of representative sermons is that they give people the space to listen, to decide, and to change; they enable the people to discover new spiritual insights and sources of strength for themselves, insights and strengths that will be valuable long after a particular congregational crisis has passed.

The Communal Model. All Christians are commissioned, in their baptism, to proclaim the gospel, in word and deed, to all the world. Each believer is in a unique position to share insights into faith. When we speak of waiting and hope at Advent, who can articulate that better than a woman who has known what it is to wait for the birth of a child? When we hear Jesus' call to the poor and powerless, who can speak of this more clearly than those who have actually known poverty?

Luther noted that whereas all Christians were called to witness and evangelize, for the sake of order some Christians would do this on Sunday morning in the assembly. The ordained preacher determines when it is fitting and proper for the other "priests" in the congregation to proclaim the word. The word that even the ordained preacher speaks is the word given to the whole church, not just to the preacher alone. In a congregational crisis, the pastor might ask, "Who is best able to preach to this particular congregation, on this particular question, at this particular time?" Is the question that is under discussion the question of whether or not to support a resolution for a nuclear arms freeze? Perhaps there is someone in the congregation or in the wider community who should speak to this, someone other than the pastor. The pastor can still be preacher as he or she is coordinating the preaching of others.

Was Paul reflecting this communal model of preaching

when he said to the Corinthians, "When you come together, each one has a hymn, a lesson, a revelation, a tongue, or an interpretation. Let all things be done for edification. If any speak in a tongue, let there be only two or at most three, and each in turn; and let one interpret. But if there is no one to interpret, let each of them keep silence in church and speak to himself and to God. Let two or three prophets speak, and let the others weigh what is said. If a revelation is made to another sitting by, let the first be silent. For you can all prophesy one by one, so that all may learn and all be encouraged; and the spirits of prophets are subject to prophets. For God is not a God of confusion but of peace" (1 Cor. 14:26–33).

In a dialogue sermon, the preacher may reflect upon some issue and then invite a public sharing of reflections on the Scripture reading within the service. Such preaching is best when the congregation is able to tolerate a high degree of informality and risk. If the sermon is opened for responses from the congregation, the pastor must exercise care to make sure that all are heard and that the time for dialogue is brought to a close after a reasonable period of reflection. Dialogue works best when the gathered assembly is small enough for everyone to hear the dialogue. Generally speaking, most congregations would quickly tire if this method were used often.

The community may be drawn into the preaching process by securing a group of parishioners to help in planning the sermons for a specific period of time. The group will meet sometime before Sunday to discuss the text and to volunteer ideas and questions that the preacher then utilizes in preparation. The pastor still prepares the sermon, but the people provide much of the substance.

Mary was serving a church that was being torn apart by a dispute over the place of charismatic gifts, specifically glossolalia, within the congregation. One group had experienced "the gift of tongues" and was now insisting that this gift be the test of the religious commitment of the other members. She felt that she ought to speak to the issue from the pulpit but frankly felt that she had an inadequate understanding of the questions and tensions involved in the issue. She randomly selected equal numbers of persons who perceived themselves to be on the opposite sides of the issue.

They were asked to meet with the pastor each week for a period of five weeks to study the scripture for the next Sunday and to reflect upon its meaning, particularly in the light of the struggle going on in the congregation.

The group learned a number of things about itself. It found that, while there were serious differences on the place of speaking in tongues within the church, there were many other issues that crossed over these divisions. The pastor, in listening to the laypersons discuss the texts, gained new insights, a host of applicable illustrations for her sermon, and a fresh commitment to her preaching.

It is possible to use such a group without centering upon a specific text. The group could consist of a representative cross section of the church membership. Generally, such groups function best when people are invited to participate for a specific period of time. Six to eight weeks is best. The leader of the group does not necessarily need to be the preacher. Responses could be tape-recorded for the minister to hear. This ensures that the minister's presence does not inhibit the group.

If the minister is present, he or she should not dominate the group. Let the minister sit quietly and take notes, perhaps asking questions for clarification from time to time. The pastor may be discouraged to learn how little relevance parishioners see in the biblical texts. But at least the pastor will approach the preaching task with new honesty about the congregation's limitations in applying scripture to its life together.

Such groups emphasize the importance of lay involvement. They make clear to the congregation that the minister really is open to the people's opinions, that the words from the pulpit are more than the pastor's own idiosyncratic ideas. Participants in the group gain a new appreciation of the difficulties inherent in preaching as well as a new commitment to preaching, since they have been an active part of the process.

The preacher who has come to a sort of mental block in preparing a sermon, or who feels that he or she has run out of relevant material for sermons, will be invigorated by the sermon discussion group. The troublesome gap between scripture and the congregation's contemporary situation will be healed. The minister's own faith will also grow in the process, stimulated by the gifts of fellow Christians who also have theological gifts that need to be utilized.

Particularly in the midst of a congregational crisis, the sermon discussion group puts the preacher in weekly contact with members of the congregation. They see their preacher in a new light, gain new understanding for the difficulties inherent in proclamation, and receive pastoral care in a new and intense way.

Some safeguards should be followed on the use of the material from the sessions. Members should be asked to identify any material they do not want used in a sermon. They should also be warned that the minister will not use all the ideas and comments from the group. I have found that such groups contribute immeasurably to the growth of my own preaching ability.

The Use of the Bible in Times of Congregational Crisis

It is assumed throughout this book that the Bible is central to the task of preaching. The Bible gives the Christian preacher his or her most enduring, appropriate material. It sets the parameters of our discourse about the church, rephrases our questions so that they are more faithful, and judges our answers.

There can be Christian sermons that are not based exclusively on the Bible. But these are a rarity. In a time of conflict within the congregation, the preacher may be tempted to answer the "What shall I preach?" question by jumping to his or her own opinions and preaching those. But this robs the preacher of the opportunity to grow in the crisis, to have the preacher's opinions and prejudices judged in the light of scripture. It also robs the congregation of its book, the book by which its life together is formed and measured.

In the congregations I have served, I have found an amazing willingness of the people to hear even painful and controversial ideas if they sense that these ideas arise from the preacher's earnest struggle to listen to their book. They may disagree with the preacher's interpretation, but at least they feel that the preacher has begun at the right place and they are struggling along with the preacher to be faithful to the text. They take pride that their preacher has been willing to stand at the intersection of the Bible and their church, willing to speak what he or she hears, even if it is a painful word. The text interprets the situation; the situation shapes the interpretation.

But biblical preaching is no easy matter. Constant care and humility are required of the biblical preacher. In confronting a text, we are tempted to resolve the distance between our concerns and those of the text by resorting to easy transference (here is what the Bible said to people in conflict then, and that's exactly what God would say to us in conflict now), eisegesis (I begin with my own preconceptions and then search for a text that superficially seems to confirm my ideas—regardless of the original context or purpose of that text), or moralizing (reduction of the biblical text into simplistic moral prescriptions, something that we are to be or to do in this current crisis).

I advocate the use of a lectionary as a source for preaching. We all have an inclination to return to our favorite passages rather than explore unfamiliar texts in our preaching. The lectionary calls our attention to elements of the gospel we might miss if left to our own devices. To pastors who are speaking to a specific congregational crisis, the lectionary may appear to be a great hindrance. We want to say something about the need for greater financial commitment because of the congregation's current budget crisis, but we find that money is not mentioned in the scripture for the next six months!

There are times, and perhaps this may be one, when we will need to forsake the lectionary in order to preach on a current situation. The lectionary is an aid to opening up a wider exposure to scripture, but it need not be a straitjacket. However, the preacher would be well advised to forsake the lectionary only after carefully studying its passages to see whether indeed these passages do relate to the crisis at hand. They may not relate in a simple, one-to-one way. But they may speak a word that we would miss if we simply pawed through the Bible looking for a simple answer to the question.

My congregation was in the throes of whether or not to support our denomination's stand against nuclear arms. It was one of the first Sundays after Pentecost. What could I say? I looked in the lectionary—the first lesson was from Genesis 1. In pondering that lesson, I realized that here was a basis for thinking about the fate of the world. The world was God's beloved creation. What God had fashioned in love should we dare to destroy? Here seemed to be an argument against nuclear war of any kind. Yet there was more for me here. Written at a time of chaos and uncertainty in Israel, the Genesis accounts of creation also wanted to proclaim that God was in charge of the world. God's great power upheld the world. God had pushed back the chaos to create the world and God's ordering love continued. Many people are simply overwhelmed by the immensity of the nuclear issue. Despair is often the result of our feeling out of control, terrified by the prospect of nuclear disaster. Our terror leads to moral paralysis. Christians affirm that this is God's world. God is on the side of order and creativity and against chaos and destruction. "The earth is the Lord's and the fulness thereof," says the psalmist. Here is an affirmation that gives us hope and confidence, even in the midst of a dangerous situation.

To me this is an example of how the Bible often teaches us to rephrase our questions. We are pragmatic, problem-solving people. But often the Bible fails to give us an answer. Rather, the Bible gives us a basis for arriving at the answer. It is often a compass, pointing us in the right direction, rather than a road map telling us exactly which turn to take next.

The Bible itself, in the midst of the congregational crises of the first churches, frequently backs off from a particular topic under discussion, reminds its hearers of the grand themes of faith, and resumes the discussion within the context of this greater theological affirmation. Fred Craddock notes that, in speaking to the Corinthians who were quarreling over the matter of whether or not to eat meat offered to idols, Paul sets the matter in a larger context by declaring, "Yet for us there is one God, the Father, from whom are all things and for whom we exist, and one Lord, Jesus Christ, through whom are all things and through whom we exist" (1 Cor. 8:6). Suddenly the theological stakes are raised. The debate is moved from a squabble over the comparatively minor matter of food offered to idols to a major issue of how well the congregation will be able to embrace the unity and greatness of God. Paul's affirmation is of such size and scope as to silence petty disputes, or at least to move beyond the present congregational crisis to a grand occasion to preach about the greatness of God.[15]

The preacher will want to put everything in perspective. The Latin root of the word "perspective" literally means "to see through." That's what the Bible offers us—an opportunity to see through the immediate to the larger issues of faith. What does the preacher say to a congregation whose problem is not the redecorating of the sanctuary or the hiring of an educational assistant but rather the paralyzing fear of the future? All petty moralisms are beside the point. The congregation might like to think that its problem is simply how to reach an agreement on the issue. But the preacher will take his or her cue from the Bible and look for those theological resources which enable us to fend off the fears that bind us. The preacher must get out of the role of answer giver and assume the role of the one who urges a continuing spiritual search whether or not this particular congregational crisis is solved.

A Tale of Two Sermons

What we preach is a function of our image of preacher and preaching task, the word we hear in our study of the scripture, and our reflections within the congregation.

Here is a pastor whose congregation is confronted with the building of a low-income housing development within sight of the church. The first reaction of the congregation was anger and fear. The members had recently finished their new educational building. Now it seemed, "Our neighborhood is being ruined." Some of the members had intimated, "We might have to start looking for another church if we are inundated by those people." When the evangelism committee suggested that the church develop a program of outreach to the inhabitants of the new housing development, matters were brought to a head. The pastor decided he must speak.

It was the middle of the season of Epiphany and the scripture text for the next Sunday was Luke 4:16–30, the familiar story of Jesus' first sermon in his hometown synagogue at Nazareth. Among the myriad of possible sermons on this familiar text, two formed in the preacher's mind. Here are synopses of the two sermons.

*   *   *

Today's scripture tells about the difficulty Jesus encountered when he tried to tell the people at Nazareth the truth about their relationship with God. I can tell you that, as a preacher, I pay lots of attention to this story. For I don't want to forget what happened to Jesus that day! I hope that you will not greet my words today the same as Jesus was greeted at Nazareth!

What Jesus did that day was to preach a good, biblical sermon. But look how people responded. They wanted to kill him when the sermon was finished. Why? Because Jesus told them two of their own beloved, familiar stories, the story of Elijah and the widow of Zarephath and the story of Elisha's healing of the Syrian, Naaman, reminding them that God had once gone to foreigners before going to the needy people in Israel.

We can imagine why that angered those Jews. Here they were in the synagogue, studying the scriptures, listening to the preacher, waiting for the Messiah. For Jesus to remind them that God might go to those whom they considered to be outsiders was anger-provoking. They wanted to kill him for implying that God could be God to the outsiders as well as to the insiders.

I don't mean to place myself in the same position of Jesus at Nazareth, but I feel that it is my duty to tell you that many of us in this congregation are guilty of the same sins that afflicted the people of Nazareth. I think you all know what I am thinking about now. I am thinking about the new housing development that has been built in such close proximity to our church. In some people's eyes, these new neighbors are not neighbors at all. They are outsiders, untouchables.

I am not going to tell you what you should do, because I think you know what Jesus would have us do. Either we can be like those narrow, closed-minded people at Nazareth or we can be the sort of people who would be a credit to Jesus. The choice is ours.

Today's scripture tells about the time that Jesus returned to his hometown to preach. We follow the story through a dramatic change of mood. Their initial pride and amazement at the beautiful, familiar words of Jesus turns to angry, murderous resentment.

As a preacher, I pay special attention to a story like this one. Any preacher wants to know what needs to be done to get the congregation to accept what he has to say, and I am no different. I identify with Jesus, looking at the people in Nazareth, wondering, What made them so angry?

That's where I like to picture myself—in the pulpit with Jesus, standing there saying, "Go get them, Jesus. I'm with you all the way!"

But that's not fair. For I am not Jesus. I am not standing with him in the pulpit, but I am sitting with you in the congregation. I am listening to this scripture with you. If you think you are made uncomfortable by hearing Jesus say that God loves even outsiders, foreigners, nonbelievers like that poor widow and that sick Syrian, imagine how I, a preacher, the resident theologian, feel! I feel uncomfortable too. As a preacher, I spend my day ministering to my own flock. You are the people who pay me, the people to whom I am accountable. More than that, I love you and want to please you and serve you. But here is Jesus reminding me that, while I may be content to serve you, my fellow brothers and sisters in Christ, God's love is even more inclusive.

This congregation is faced with nearby "outsiders," people who are somewhat akin to the poor widow and the sick Syrian whom God's prophets healed. We are fearful—I am fearful—of what their presence might mean. Will our beloved congregation be changed? Will these newcomers try to take us over and change us over into their image? Will they even like us, or will they see us as a cold, aloof, self-centered group of people? What will these new neighbors mean to me as a pastor?

Here I sit, with you, in the pew, listening to a story about how Jesus managed to threaten and eventually anger a congregation by reminding them that God's love often goes over our boundaries.

I'm a pastor. I'm supposed to be able to love everybody. God has called me into a ministry of preaching, teaching, and care for all of God's children. Will I be able to be that good pastor? Will these newcomers reveal to me my limitations as a good preacher, a faithful pastor, an all-embracing caregiver? I hear Jesus say what he says in today's scripture, and my fears rise and my fears will eventually develop into anger, for that's usually the way fear turns out.

I want to hear Jesus, but I also want to be honest about my fears, my limitations. Will you help me try to listen to what Jesus wants to preach to me in this situation? Let us listen together, in the hope that we might be given the faith to move beyond our fear, to be bold in our discipleship, and thus one day to proclaim, even in our beloved little congregation, "This is the acceptable time of the Lord."

*		*		*

Two sermons on the same text, but note how they differ. Note the posture of the preachers. In one, the preacher is looking down upon the congregation from the pulpit, asking the congregation to come up and join him in looking down upon these new "foreigners." The first sermon implies that the preacher knows what ought to be done and is quite willing to do it if only this stubborn congregation would get serious and follow him. The second sermon honestly confesses the minister's own misgivings and struggle. It is easy for a preacher to stand up and pontificate about reaching out to these newcomers. But in reaching out, the members may permanently change the identity of a beloved congregation. There is much at stake for both the preacher and the congregation and the second sermon tries to be honest about some of these fears. Will his confession free others in the congregation to struggle?

In the first sermon, the preacher is clearly detached from the congregation. In the second sermon, the preacher is sitting there beside the people as they struggle together with a difficult text made even more difficult by their difficult congregational crisis. If any of them are fearful and therefore angry, they all are fearful and angry together. The minister's superior posture in the first sermon implies superior intelligence, commitment, and power. There is no measure of weakness or wrongness, just rightness. In the second sermon, it is clear that the minister is with the congregation in a mutual effort to be faithful to Jesus.

In deciding what to preach, the pastor goes to the scripture. But the pastor arrives at the scripture's word with the words of the congregation: What does this text have to say to us today? Will it cost us something? How will I look after the operation? Will the preacher listen with me to the scripture, or does the preacher only want to tell me what I am supposed to do?

In these questions, as the sermon begins to form, the sacred roles of preacher, prophet, representative, and community person merge as one, and the tense, Monday morning question, "What should I preach?" becomes the more pastoral, *"How* should I preach?"

Is Preaching Effective?

Earlier we noted that there are many congregational crises that do not lend themselves to treatment from the pulpit. The pastor must decide whether a particular issue lends itself to a biblical-homiletical approach in a sermon or whether it needs to be dealt with in another setting through means other than the sermon.

But a larger issue is behind the question of effectiveness. We preachers like to think of ourselves as effective in the pulpit, that we do actually influence the lives of our hearers. Presumably, we choose to speak to a congregational problem from the pulpit because we believe that our words can make a difference. For change to occur in human beings, two things are needed: an experiential-intellectual confrontation with the word of God and an ability to provide those conditions whereby people might be free to grow and change. Sermons "work" because those conditions are met. They fail to take root and to produce fruit because we have not met these two essential conditions.

We pastors have good reason to be somewhat skeptical of our positive assessment of our ability to influence our congregations through preaching. Many of us have a virtually magical view of preaching, that is, we think that by merely quoting the right scripture, or stating the truth clearly and engagingly, people will change. Sometimes people tell us that they have changed because of our preaching. But we usually hear this from those members of the congregation who like us and who respond positively to us and our sermons. Even those who don't like us, if directly confronted by us, will feel called upon to say something positive, such as, "Well, you gave us a lot to think about and I did like what you have to say." Most of them will simply sit there in smiling silence. Their positive comments and noncommittal silence enable us preachers to delude ourselves. We grow expert at molding our rationalizations out of our guesses about the value of our preaching. Besides, if it can be shown that people are not moved by our preaching, we can say that is because they are ignorant, uncommitted, or even perverse to the truth.

Unfortunately for our delusions, there is much empirical evidence to suggest that people are rarely fundamentally changed by a sermon. This isn't due only to there being so few good sermons, it is due also to a basic reality of human nature. Human beings have an unconscious resistance to self-awareness and change. In fact, the more persuasive and forceful the presentation of a new awareness, the more strongly people will unconsciously resist the insight. Psychotherapists have long expressed amazement at the tenacity and persistence of our mechanisms for resistance. The patient may claim that he or she wants to find answers, to change life for the better, to face the facts even if they hurt, but then will unconsciously rationalize, excuse, or deflect any attempt to change.

If we listen to scripture, we find that the response to early Christian preaching was decidedly mixed. Not everyone responded with an enthusiastic "Amen!" Paul even got so disgusted with some of the intransigence of his congregation at Galatia that he called them a bunch of fools (see Gal. 3:1). While a superficial listening to scripture suggests that every early congregation lived in peace and perfection, careful, honest exegetical attention to the text reveals that conflict, rejection, and disagreement were part of that experience.

Should we give up on preaching? No! We should simply chasten our enthusiasm by an honest assessment of the limits of any method, including preaching, in changing the hearts and minds of people. We cannot make people face the truth. But we can facilitate, fail to facilitate, or even impede the openness of persons to the word of God when it is spoken. The soil can be prepared for the seed. How we speak can either raise defenses in a person or open windows to fresh breezes of the Spirit.

Listening to our own motives as we preach and listening to God's people in our own congregation help us honestly to accept what preaching cannot do while boldly anticipating what preaching can do.

6

Listening to Text
and Context

When we hear the word "preaching," we think of speaking, public speaking, public speaking done in church. Perhaps we pastors would be on safer ground to think of preaching as listening. Much of our preaching fails, not because we have not spoken well, but because we have listened so poorly. Take Sarah, for instance.

Sarah came to St. Luke's as pastor about two years ago. Even though she followed a beloved pastor who had been there for nearly twenty years, things began well. The congregation seemed willing and eager to make a fresh start of things. At first she didn't mind hearing, "Pastor Dave always did it this way." She knew that some amount of this was to be expected. Gradually the references to Pastor Dave and his way of doing things began to annoy her.

After her first year, it seemed as though "the honeymoon" was over. The people seemed to be much more critical of her style of leadership. Some complained that she didn't visit enough or that her sermons were "too intellectual." She was bothered by an apparent decline in attendance. Above all, she was greatly annoyed at the difficulty the nominating committee had faced in finding people to serve on the church's various committees. Person after person declined to serve. By the third depressing meeting of the nominating committee, she was really discouraged.

Sarah determined to preach on the problem of the wavering commitment in the congregation. She took as her text the account of the great banquet in Luke 14:15–24. It seemed a perfect text for her purposes. After all, wasn't the problem in the congregation that many professed that they wanted to support the church, wanted to participate in its work and fellowship, but when the invitation came for them to accept responsibility, they made silly excuses? Just as there were people in the parable who refused the invitation to the great banquet, so there were many in the congregation who "all alike began to make excuses" (Luke 14:18). The title of her sermon was "Excuses, Excuses." As an example of our excuse-making tendencies, she frankly shared her deep disappointment over the failure of the nominating committee to complete its work because of the lack of positive response from the persons whom it wished to nominate.

As she ended her sermon that Sunday, Sarah said, "Jesus says, 'I tell you, none of those . . . who were invited shall taste my banquet.' The pitiful sight of those hungry people standing on the outside of the banquet hall is a frightening warning to each of us. Have we allowed the unimportant things of life to crowd out the important things? Excuses? Excuses?"

Sarah had hoped, through this sermon, to motivate the congregation to greater commitment and participation. What was the result? First, people really did seem to hear her frustration. On the way out of church, more than one person attempted to say something supportive such as, "I know that it's discouraging for a young person like you to understand a group of old folks like us. Please be patient." Someone else said, "It's a real shame that people have just gotten so overcommitted, these days." She assumed that this meant that some had heard and had agreed with her.

There were some apparently negative responses. One person told her, as she waited in the hallway after church, "Well, I guess I was one of the ones you were preaching to. I said no to the committee because I'm sick and tired of the same people always having to do all the work around here." There were other, less straightforward responses, but Sarah got the definite impression that people were either resentful or hurt by her sermon.

She decided to share the experience with a group of colleagues who met for coffee and conversation each Monday morning. Through that conversation, Sarah was able to gain some distance and perspective on the episode. She eventually came to these conclusions about the sermon and its results:

Had she really preached to the situation within the congregation? She was frustrated and she apparently conveyed that to her hearers. But did she also convey her anger and fear? Things had been going so well. Now the honeymoon was over. Were things going to fall apart? Perhaps, she reasoned, their excuses were their way of registering their displeasure over the direction of the congregation—like rats leaving a sinking ship! Perhaps she had moved much too fast with her changes. A year seemed like a long time to wait for them to "get over" Pastor Dave. But was it realistic of her to expect their grief and readjustment at the termination of a twenty-year pastorate to be over so soon?

Unfortunately her sermon preparation and presentation left little room for these questions. She had decided that the problem was a rather simple one of lack of Christian commitment. These people had claimed that they wanted to follow Jesus, but look at their silly excuses! Thus she implied that those who said no to the committee were something less than committed Christians. She failed to speak to the possible complexity of feeling among the congregation or within herself. In fact, she commented later that she learned a great deal more about her congregation after the sermon than before. Post-sermon dialogue can be significant. But it might have been more significant if she had done more skillful listening to herself and to the congregation before she preached.

Rather than preach as one who is in the midst of the struggle to be a faithful church, Sarah had placed herself above the battle. She was the preacher, looking down upon all the uncommitted half-Christians, pointing out their half-hearted commitment. Such preaching drives a wedge between pastor and people, because the persons who have been justly accused may become even more defensive and those who have been unjustly accused may be deeply resentful that the pastor has misread their feelings and motives.

Even more surprising for Sarah was the realization that she might have also failed to hear the biblical text. Are the excuses offered for the great banquet silly or serious? Commentators disagree. But what if the excuses are far from frivolous? Land was at a premium in the Near East (Luke

14:18) and a prudent person would need to take care in the purchase of property. Livestock was a matter of life and death to a family (Luke 14:19), and thus a loving householder surely must care for his oxen. Isn't marriage always an appropriate subject for serious commitment? Who can blame the new groom for wanting to start out his marriage right (Luke 14:20)? Perhaps Jesus knows that the reasons that keep us away from the kingdom are rarely frivolous. The conflict is not between good and bad but between competing goods. Discipleship is therefore a most difficult matter of setting priorities and making choices between one good thing and another. It is tough, and preachers ought not to make the choices to appear simpler than they really are.

We should also note that Jesus chose to talk about the invitation to discipleship through a story, a parable that entices us into its dilemma. In so doing, the parable enables us to let our defenses down, to see ourselves in the lives of others, to hear things that we would not have heard any other way. But Sarah chose to speak in a straightforward, moralistic fashion. Jesus did not prescribe any behavior. He merely told a story and then gave his hearers room to draw their own conclusions on the basis of what they heard. Sarah gave them no such freedom; rather, she put herself in the place of the scolding parent who tells the wayward children what to do. Thus there are questions of both content and style in her treatment of the passage.

Fortunately for her congregation, Sarah is a secure and competent enough pastor to seek out and to hear the criticisms of her peers. She grew in this experience, and her congregation will be better for it. Her example strikes a chord in all of us, for we all have been where she was—busy speaking to a congregation on a perplexing issue without first having taken the time to listen either to the congregational context or to the biblical text.

Listening to the Context

Communication does not occur in a vacuum. Every time you preach, you speak within an ecology of a distinctive parish. Meaningful preaching occurs in those contexts when a preacher has learned to listen.

"Get inside the minds of your hearers," Spurgeon told preachers of his day. In order to do that, you must get inside their homes, schools, offices, and factories, their nursing homes and prison cells. Earlier we spoke of a pastor's ecclesiastically bestowed authority to preach. But we must here admit that a preacher's authority is also earned. People listen to one who has skillfully listened to them. None of us enjoys being treated as an object, a type, or a class. We desire to be known in our individuality, our specificity. As a pastor, you are in a wonderful position to listen, to know your people by name, to sit where they sit and think as they think.

When do you begin to compose a sermon? For most pastors, that question is difficult to answer. Some of our best thoughts arise while we are at the bedside in the hospital or hurrying from one meeting to the next or in the midst of a counseling session. We are always gathering material, exposing ourselves to the life situations that make preaching lively and significant.

Listening is important for any sermon, but particularly important for a sermon that presumes to speak to a congregational problem. People do not listen to what you have to say if they feel that you have not taken the trouble to listen to them. Sarah discovered that she had jumped to quick conclusions about "the problem" in her church. In reality, the problem that she diagnosed as "a lack of real Christian commitment" was much more interesting and complicated. The resistance that the nominating committee encountered may have arisen not from a simple lack of commitment but rather from the people's very deep, very real commitment to their church. They were committed to *their* church, the church they had loved, the church which Pastor Dave had given them, and here was this new, young pastor trying to take their church away from them. Now, they fought her out of their strong commitment to let their church be their church.

Sarah also failed to hear their continuing grief. When she encountered the fond references to dear Pastor Dave, Sarah heard a challenge to her power, her future authority. Did the people really mean these references the way Sarah was interpreting them? There is no way to answer that question except through careful listening.

The distinguished Swedish sociologist Gunnar Myrdal once remarked that there is no such thing as an economic problem, there are only problems. We are fond of labeling the mysteries of life in the congregation as "power struggles," "lack of faith," "disorganization," and so forth. A pastor is in the position of discovering that parish problems are multidimensional, complex, and interesting.

A church is not a book club. A book club will have problems, but rarely do they become as vicious and intense as problems within the church. The person who is perplexed that people behave so nicely at his or her book club but seem to fight like cats and dogs at church need not be so baffled. In the church, we are dealing with ultimate questions, our very deepest needs. Even though we may not state that the dispute over the placement of furniture in the church parlor is really a dispute over our relationship to God, that may be why this seemingly petty fight becomes so vicious.

So, as you start to prepare for preaching about a local church problem, begin by carefully listening and analyzing what you hear. Follow the same type of procedure you use when a couple come to you for counseling about their marriage problem. You must carefully listen, ask the right questions, and try to discern the dynamics of the situation, the hidden and unspoken agenda, the fears that are leading to their anxiety and anger. After you have listened to them, you must speak a word of diagnosis. In like fashion, your sermon is your diagnosis of the conflict that currently troubles your congregation.

Victor Borge tells of a crackpot physician who prescribed the same cure for every illness. An aunt of his had a cold, took the doctor's prescription, and died of the cure! As ministers to the internal health of our congregations, we must take care to make the proper diagnosis in order to offer the proper prescription.

A friend of mine was serving a church that was bitterly divided over whether or not to build a new sanctuary or to continue worshiping in the multipurpose gymnasium–fellowship hall. In the early days of the debate, he had refrained from taking a stand or expressing his point of view. After all, he knew that, if the sanctuary was going to be built, it would have to be built with the laypeople's money and they would have to be solidly behind the project. But the debate seemed to be forming into two warring camps, each with its own solidly entrenched point of view. It was here that he decided to speak to the issue in a sermon.

Before speaking, he decided to go through a careful, intentional process of listening to the different factions on the issue. He found that some members felt that an expensive sanctuary was a needless extravagance and a waste of the congregation's limited resources. These people had always taken pride in saying, "Our congregation is not a fancy, rich group of people." The bare, utilitarian fellowship hall was a symbol of the simplicity, youthful vitality, and humble nature of the congregation. They were unmoved by the others' argument that the church now needed a new sanctuary in order to attract new members. These people thought the church was large enough already.

He found that those on the other side felt that the meager fellowship hall reflected negatively upon the congregation. "Aren't you ashamed that we all live in relatively fine homes but are content to worship God in this gymnasium?" they asked. The gymnasium was fine when their children were young. But now their children were old enough to be thinking about weddings and they were old enough to be thinking about funerals and the thought of having weddings and funerals in the fellowship hall displeased them greatly. Their concern was not only aesthetic. Many of these people felt that the church needed a new challenge, the same sort of challenge they had felt when the first building was erected. A fund-raising drive for a new sanctuary would be the perfect means of mobilizing the congregation.

As he talked to the people, he found himself leaning toward those who wanted a new sanctuary. At first he resisted the notion—probably because he couldn't bear the thought of a long and difficult building program and because he knew that such a campaign would cause conflict in the congregation. He felt that he had enough challenges and problems within the church now without taking on new ones. Yet he thought that a new sanctuary would present a better image to the surrounding neighborhood. He too was growing tired of worshiping in a setting that he felt was unsuitable for Christian worship at its best. It could mean a great deal to the morale of the congregation to have a more attractive worship space.

So he began by being honest with himself: He really did have a point of view, a position within the conflict, and it would be more honest of him to admit it to himself and to the people. Yet what effect would this have on the people who disagreed?

He sat down in his study and made a list of the leading voices on each side of the argument. There were many in the congregation who frankly didn't know which side they were on. They would be the most receptive to a sermon on the subject as a means of helping them to make up their minds. Who were those who adamantly opposed the idea of the new sanctuary? He listed their names and tried to imagine what arguments they might make, how they might respond to a sermon on the subject, what he might say to them that would enable them to see things differently.

This stage was an important one in the process of sermon preparation. It kept the preacher from seeing the conflict as a mere conflict about ideas and means. It reminded him that there were real flesh-and-blood people out there who loved the church and could be hurt, perhaps permanently damaged, if the issue was handled poorly. By keeping their faces in his mind as he wrote the sermon, he was better able to state his position in a way that might be more persuasive than confrontational.

Empathetic imagination is a valuable asset for any preaching, the ability to hear a word as the people in the pew might hear it. This homiletical empathy is utterly essential when one is trying to speak to a crisis. Empathy need not blunt the preacher's prophetic thrust. Rather, in empathetic listening, the preacher is able to discover who the real enemy is and where the real battle lines are drawn. Before launching into the sermon, the preacher asks, "What is it like to love this tattered old gymnasium as the very house of God, to have prayed in it for the last ten years, heard sermons here, been moved to tears during the singing of hymns?" In discussing the question of whether or not to build the new sanctuary, the pastor wanted to be fair to his people, in no way to imply that they were bad Christians because they took the opposite view on this issue. Yet he did want them to hear him and possibly change their minds.

At first he considered a sermon that said in effect, "Here are the two sides of the issue as I see them. I'm not going to tell you what I think you ought to do, since it is your decision."

But as he pictured those dozen or so faces of the persons who thought the sanctuary was a bad idea, he felt that they would resent his fence-straddling. It would be better to tell them how he sees the issue now that he has thought about all the facets of the question. But he wanted to tell them in a way that would not close out all future debate. After all, even if they decided to build, there were dozens of decisions yet to be made, many opportunities for debate and compromise. The challenge he faced would be honestly to state his opinion on the matter without suggesting that the issue was now closed.

Note the importance of the preacher's attempt to define carefully what it was he wanted to do to his hearers in the sermon. We may be somewhat squeamish about the idea that we are trying to do something to our hearers in the sermon. Such use smacks of manipulation. But it is difficult to imagine any sermon that is worth listening to that does not have a clear and steady aim of doing something to or for its listeners. If we are not yet sure of an issue and simply want to equivocate and take off of our shoulders the responsibility for a decision, we ought to admit it in the beginning rather than confuse our listeners as they rummage about in our thoughts trying to decide what it was we really wanted to say. If we are really trying to move our hearers to some point of view, let that point of view be stated now, up front, at an early stage in our sermon preparation. Let it be written in large letters across the top of the first page of our outline; let us keep it before us as we collect material, select scripture, and seek illustrations. A sermon must be aimed if it is to hit a target. Let the pastor admit and articulate to himself or herself, early in the process of preparation, that he or she really does want to do something to the hearers through this sermon.

As this pastor listened to people discuss both sides of the issue, he was at times troubled that they seemed to see this

as purely a matter of dollars and cents or how the church
would look to the rest of the community or how many seats
they needed in a new building. Rarely were theological
concerns introduced into the discussion. As a pastor, he felt
that raising these concerns was his proper duty. At heart, it
seemed to be a debate, not simply about two buildings, but
about the very nature of the church itself, about discipleship, about how best to serve and witness for Jesus Christ
in this place.

For his sermon, he took as the text the familiar story of
Mary and Martha when Jesus came to their home. Here, he
said, were two different images of discipleship. One was not
necessarily superior to the other. Both had their place. Both
women were friends of Jesus, trying to be his disciples and
to serve him faithfully. This congregation, in its past, has
been a congregation of activists, busy serving the community, reaching out to the youth and children of the young
families in the neighborhood. This should never be lost.
But there is another aspect of service to Christ—worship.
Adoration, the sheer joy of being in the presence of God,
is also a part of life in the church. Is there a way that, in this
congregation, we can bring Mary and Martha together? Can
we now turn to this rather neglected aspect of Christian life
and think about a new sanctuary? This congregation has
diversity. There are some here who look and act more like
Martha. Others fit the description of Mary. Both groups are
needed. Both are important for full, faithful discipleship in
this church.

Because the preaching and the hearing that occur in a
sermon are a holy act, the very basis of faith and the birth-
place of the church, preaching must not insult, violate, or
ignore those whose investment in the message is no less
than that of the speaker. Sermons are not generalized
speeches for all occasions but are prepared for a particular
group of people at a particular time and place. The listeners
must be able to see themselves as participants in the sermon
before it is born. It is never enough that the sermon be
generally true; rather, it must be recognizably true for these
people in their time of crisis. What you are doing, in preaching to them, is helping the listeners to interpret themselves,
to hold their lives under the light of the judgment and
blessing which is the gospel.

We also listen to the congregation because we want our sermons to be heard in such a way that listeners are moved to think, feel, decide, and act upon something because of the sermon. Generations of Christians have been conditioned to hear the sermon as a little message from the pastor, all tied up in a bow and handed to them before the last hymn. The task is simply to listen and understand, not to act. Pastors become depressed because their congregations seem so passive. But many of our sermons make them that way. One reason why the preacher wants to leave things a bit open-ended, with something left to their imaginations, is so they will be forced to finish the sermon for themselves, in their own lives. They have been conditioned through years of quiet submission to accept someone else's opinions without any risk or investment of their own.

In the sermon on Mary and Martha, the pastor left room for the listeners to walk about within the sermon. Who am I—Mary or Martha? Which aspect of faithfulness do I most closely resemble and how might my life be more fully expressive of the fullness of the gospel? As in so many of Jesus' parables, the hearers are not told, "Here is what you ought to do," but rather, "He who has ears to hear, let him hear." Dogmatic, paternalistic, propositional preaching renders a congregation either passive or resistant. We respect the abilities and commitments of our listeners when we want to entrust something to them to hear and do after the sermon is finished rather than figuring it all out for them in the sermon.

Fred Craddock first called to my attention that sermons must speak *for* as well as *to* the congregation. When we preach from the Bible, we are opening up the community's book, not the preacher's private possession. Jesus shocked the people at Nazareth (Luke 4:16–30) to a great extent because he preached to them from their own scripture. The preacher's task is not to bring to the people some new and strange word they have not yet heard but to remind them of what they already know. We are not to soothe and flatter them with what they want to *hear* but rather to articulate for them what they want to *say*.

On the way out of church they may say, "You really preached to me today," when what they mean is, "You really preached *for* me today." It is a great compliment to be told by the people that you were able to preach the sermon they would have preached if they could have. This is a blessed event, particularly in time of congregational crisis—that our preacher has come forth with our word, the word that gives this congregation vitality and strength to encounter our problems with the word of God to guide us.

In the daily listening to and living with the congregation, the pastor learns the subtleties of how this congregation goes about its business. This is that intangible but deeply significant matter of style. A sermon is characterized by a certain communicative style, the way the preacher approaches and delivers the message. Congregations also have a style, and sermons are more easily heard by a congregation when they are delivered in a style that is congruent with that congregation's way of dealing with issues.

For instance, I went into my first parish after seven years of college and seminary, trained in the methods of abstract reasoning and philosophical analysis. My first sermons tended to be analytical in nature: Here is a problem, along with two or three possible solutions, and here is the solution which I think the Bible and the Christian faith put forward. Problem—analysis—solution. Should we build a new sanctuary? Here is the problem, then three possible alternatives, followed by the only reasonable solution as I see it.

This style is fine when one is dealing with people who are accustomed to solving their problems in this way. A white-collar congregation of corporate managers would probably respond quite well to this style, since it is the style in which they work each day. But my little congregation in rural Georgia was left out in the cold. How did they solve problems? At a meeting, whenever some significant issue was being discussed, someone invariably responded by telling a story, a history lesson: "Well, this same thing came up back in the 1950s. Back then, Joe and Sarah Smith said that we ought to give it a try. We did, but we got nowhere. I don't think we would get anywhere with this today. So I am against it," she would say.

Such narrative reasoning went against my rational inclinations. I wanted to sort out competing ideas and, through a process of rational analysis, come to a conclusion. But here was a congregation that reasoned the way families often do—through storytelling, narrative, recollection, history. For them, this congregation was not a corporation; it was a story, a family living out a story. Whatever we decided to do or not to do in this situation would either continue the line of the story or disrupt it.

Therefore any sermonic attempt to speak to a problem in such a congregation would do well to follow this same narrative style. The people who were deciding whether or not to build a new sanctuary found themselves telling two different versions of the same story. In his sermon, the pastor took note of this and laid alongside the congregation's story a story from the Bible. This led to a possible revision of the congregational story in order to take account of the biblical narrative.

No sermon begins when the Bible is opened and the day's text is read. Nor does the sermon end when the preacher sits down and the last hymn is sung. Every sermon should be a long, continuous process of communication and relationship that must be pastoral if it is to be effective. Sermons have a better chance of being heard if the preacher is able to demonstrate, in the sermon, that he or she has first listened.

Listening to the Text

Giving time and attention to the interpretation of the congregational context in no way diminishes the importance of careful exegesis and hermeneutics of texts. But it reminds us that we listen to the scriptures not as disinterested academicians but as those hungry for a word to enable the church to be the church. The Bible is the result of that long conversation between God and God's chosen people. Without that word to undergird and to set the agenda for our preaching, we really have nothing to say to the church. Our opinions on various issues may be interesting. We may be entertaining in our notions. But the Bible tells us what is at stake in our congregational problems, what to value, what to seek.

Because the biblical story functions in this way for the church, the church calls its Bible its "canon," its rule for faith and practice. The canonization of scripture was no arbitrary matter. The Bible became our authority for the pastoral reason that, over the years, the community realized that here was the story that sustained its very life. Through no other story did Christians find themselves transformed. Through no other story was this promised community of love and hope made a reality.

In the midst of a congregational problem, biblical sermons help us to put the problem in context. We are not the first to have struggled to live the faith and to embody it in our life together. A preacher in the midst of a conflict ought to be encouraged when reading Paul's statement, "I entreat Euodia and I entreat Syntyche to agree in the Lord" (Phil. 4:2). When we read of the struggles of the faith community before us, we can take heart that we are not the first to fail at forming a truly faithful community and we can receive hope that God does not desert us even in the church's failures to be the church.

The Bible tells us not only what to preach when we are in the midst of a crisis but also how to preach. In preaching to local church problems we are using a vast, creative body of literature that is itself a response to local church problems. How does the Bible preach? Not *what* does it preach, but *how* does it preach? The story of Mary and Martha was told to the early church as a response to some issue in the church. How sad to take that interesting little story and convert it into three dull propositions about the nature of discipleship.

When Paul encountered problems with factionalism at First Church Corinth, he lifted up the Lord's Supper and its one loaf as a promise of what the Corinthians could become. When Luke encountered a bickering church of insiders and outsiders he told a story of a great banquet at which those whom the world judged as insiders eventually ended up out in the cold. A problem of persecution and hopelessness for the struggling little church? Mark depicts a Lord and Savior who cares for his little band of followers by commanding even the wind and the sea to do his bidding. As we listen to the text, the persistent exegetical question for us is, Does the sermon say and do to its listeners what the biblical text said and did to its original listeners? This is a far more complex matter than simply defining a problem and then assembling a string of biblical quotes which, at least at first glance, appear to relate to the problem. It may be that a sermon that constantly refers to the Bible will be "unbiblical" in the sense that it fails to deal with truth in the way that the text deals with the truth. What we want to do, in preaching from the Bible, is to unleash the text, to allow it to do its work among the people of our congregation.

Rarely does the Bible flex its muscle and cram some dogmatic assertion down our throats. More often, it draws upon our imagination rather than our fear of intimidation. Elizabeth Achtemeier has observed that we often note with amazement that people become more kind and considerate at Christmastime. Why? Perhaps because that is the season when the church puts aside its dry moralism and goes pictorial, when its high-handed "principles" and dead-letter doctrines are exchanged for shepherds kneeling on the straw and wonderful stars shining in thousands of crèches throughout the land. The poetic vision is made our story and we are transformed, charmed into being better than we are.

Too often, when we encounter an issue that we wish to treat in a sermon, we go rummaging around in scripture for just the right idea to suit our preconceived solution for the problem. But sometimes the preacher will be surprised by the Bible's treatment of the issue. Our questions will become rearranged for us by the way the Bible deals with conflict.

During the Vietnam War, my congregation was deeply divided on the church's stance toward the war and toward draft evaders. Some said, "My country, right or wrong, my country." Others felt that the war was a travesty and quoted Peter when he stood before the governing authorities and said, "We must obey God rather than men."

The preacher turned for help to Paul's remarks about the "governing authorities." Did not Paul say that we were to obey those who were placed over us in positions of authority in our government?

After carefully studying the passage, he came to a very different conclusion. Paul did advocate obeying governmental authorities as well as urging slaves to obey their masters. Why? Was it that the authorities have divinely given power and should be obeyed at all cost and slaves have no right to question their masters? The church has interpreted these texts in this way on occasion.

No. Paul looked forward to the end of the world within his own lifetime. In his view, one could go ahead and obey the governing authorities, not because they had power and influence but because they have already been disarmed and rendered irrelevant by what the church knows in Jesus Christ. A Christian can freely obey these Roman governors because they are really of very little account in the eyes of God, who has sent a new king who is not Caesar to rule over us.

This does not answer what a Christian ought to do in specific instances of conflict between the church and the government, but it does shed new light on the relationship between church and state. It does set up the argument in a more Christian way, moving us away from dull and conventional arguments about patriotism and nationalism toward concern for faithfulness in our time and place.

The movement back from the study of the text to the congregational context thus helps us to see "the problem" in a new light. We are again placed in dialogue with scripture in a way that demands that we rephrase and relocate our questions. Admittedly, such preaching is easier to desire than to achieve. It would be simpler to nod in the direction of the text and then push ahead to the solution one already had in mind. In listening to the text, we may expect surprises.

7

How Will They Respond?

When I became pastor at one church, a number of people mentioned that the former pastor preached children's sermons every Sunday. About midway through the service, he would call the children to the front, tell them a short story, and have a prayer. Then they would be taken out to some activity in the basement. Why did I not preach children's sermons? I tried to explain myself to those who asked, telling them about my theological, developmental, and liturgical objections to children's sermons. I also admitted that I simply did not do them very well. My concern was to find ways more fully to integrate children into every aspect of worship, to keep them with us throughout the entire Sunday morning service. After the matter came up in the congregation's worship committee, I felt that I needed to speak about the subject from the pulpit.

My opportunity to preach about children in the church came a few Sundays later when the epistle lesson was from Romans 12 where Paul uses the analogy of the body to speak of the various parts of the church. Focusing my sermon on Paul's idea that those members of the body which we might regard as "inferior" are given great honor by God (Rom. 12:14–24), I spoke on the central place of children within our church and our need to welcome them warmly into all the activities of our church. I also stated why I thought children's sermons, in spite of our well-meaning intentions, did not really speak to children.

During the week after I preached the sermon it became evident that here was a sermon that was not well received.

To my surprise, many people seemed to hear the opposite
of what I thought I was trying to say. Some heard the sermon as a retreat from the church's concern for children.
Children's sermons were viewed as the primary way to show
our care for children and, if we did away with children's
sermons, no matter what else we did, we were still not doing
enough.

Others heard the sermon as a nonsensical call to turn the
church over to the children. "I don't care what you say, you
don't know what it's like to try to sit with three kids and
worship. My children don't belong there during the whole
service and I am not going to insist that they stay," one
mother said to me. Others worried that the children would
be restless, would disrupt the concentration and meditation
of the adults, and so forth.

I could live with their disagreement. I could accept that
we had a fundamental difference of opinion. I could also
understand that these attitudes did not arise overnight and
that they would not be changed overnight. But I did hope
that, at least among some of them, their minds would
change. Why did so few seem to change as a result of my
sermon? What could I have said differently? More to the
point perhaps, *How* could I have said it differently?

The people's response to my sermon on children is not
a particularly surprising or original example of what happens when a preacher attempts to speak to a congregational
problem. And that's just the point. We encounter such response, or lack of response, quite often. People either seem
to hear the very opposite of what we thought we were
preaching or they adamantly refuse to agree with what we
believe to be a perfectly logical and acceptable point of
view.

If a pastor preaches on local church problems, that
preacher had better be prepared for resistance and rejection of his or her message. Why do people not hear what we
say? Are there ways in which we can adjust our methods and
means of preaching to increase the possibility of acceptance
of our message?

Hearing but Not Hearing

Long ago, psychotherapists noted that people have difficulty hearing painful, potentially threatening information. In spite of our declaration that we are listening, that we really want to hear, that we are open to change, we have a wide array of unconscious defenses with which we block and resist data that threaten us. To accomplish change in our listeners, we must first be heard. Psychotherapy's observations of the ways in which resistance functions, as well as the factors that contribute to successful communication, are valuable insights for the preacher. In preaching to problems within the parish, I do not aim simply to present information but rather to accomplish transformation. While preaching is not therapy, a therapist's insights can inform our preaching method.

It is natural for us to erect various means of self-protection as a reaction to people who try to change us. This is a healthy response of ego protection. Kierkegaard learned that information alone does not produce change. Something else must be needed. When people are confronted directly, they put up walls, walls that are thoroughly resistant to the preacher's efforts to batter them down. Resistance is the result of our unconscious attempt to maintain our psychic status quo.

The preacher may encounter resistance in the congregation where people huddle on all the back seats rather than come to the front, near the pulpit. Or large numbers of people may always arrive late, wel after the service has begun. A decline in attendance, particularly if that decline can be correlated with a change in the congregation or a particular matter under discussion, can be a sign of resistance. Through these seemingly unrelated behaviors, people may be expressing their unconscious reaction to potentially disruptive ideas from the pulpit.

Or resistance may be more verbal and overt. People may abruptly dismiss what we say without appearing to think seriously. When we state something in a sermon, as clearly and directly as we know how, and our listeners hear the exact opposite, their inability to hear may arise from an unconscious unwillingness to hear. Or people may ignore our words and attack us instead. Repression, projection, displacement, intellectualization, and avoidance are all defense mechanisms in service of shutting out what they do not want to hear.

When therapists encounter resistance, they learn to respect it as a powerful psychological force that is never easily overcome. They know that resistance is particularly resilient to direct, frontal assault. Every therapist develops certain skills in approaching resistance. One skill is the development of a relationship with the client. Throughout this book we have noted the importance of the development of a spirit of trust between pastor and congregation. Trust in the pastor, developed through a wide range of encounters within the daily life of the congregation, is the most important factor in pastoral communication.

Unlike most therapy, preaching is more than two-way communication. Roger Fallot reminds us that God is also a party in this conversation. Whereas therapy may dissolve when problems are not resolved or when the therapist and the client come to a painful impasse in their conversation, if the relationship between preacher and congregation "is cast in the light of their shared responsibility before God, a different understanding of cooperation between the preacher and congregation develops."[16] In sermons on subjects of congregational concern, resistance may be minimized by placing potential conflicts, not between the preacher and the congregation, but between God's will or intentions on the one hand and the preacher and congregation on the other.

The preacher will want to make clear that the sermon is an effort to discern God's intention and that the preacher is dependent upon God's grace and judgment as much as the congregation. It must be clear that the one who stands in the pulpit is also the one who is able to sit next to the people in the pew.

But even this relationship between pastor and people is no guarantee that the sermon will not be resisted. It is important that the preacher know that the client may be resistant and that the preacher empathize with that resistance. In chapter 5, the second sermon on Jesus in the synagogue at Nazareth was more effective because the preacher let the people know that he identified with their fears and misgivings.

We are not depicting the congregation as full of potential adversaries or suggesting that the listeners are not hearing because they do not like the preacher. Such perception becomes a self-fulfilling prophecy. As Fallot says, "If congregational resisting is not viewed as oppositional, . . but as intelligible misgivings about the possible call for personal change, new preaching possibilities emerge "[17] Empathy undermines the adversarial stance as the preacher explores his or her common bond with the listeners. The sermon becomes an attempt to understand the listeners, not simply to overcome their misgivings.

Acknowledging and expressing ambivalent or resistant feelings is a first step toward overcoming resistance. The preacher is moved from self-righteous accusation to acknowledgment. In speaking to the problem of what to do about children in worship, the preacher refrains from saying, "If you really cared about children, as so many of you claim, then . . . ." Instead, the preacher might recall his or her own childhood experiences and memories, positive and negative, of church. What influences contributed to his or her early religious development? Such reflection might free others in the congregation to explore their memories and thus to open up to fresh thinking on the subject.

The pastor is troubled that the congregation is willing to invest great amounts of money in its own building and facilities but is resistant to giving its full share to the denominational mission program. The first plan for a sermon that begins in shame for the lavish church building when compared to, say, the plight of a hungry child in Mexico is replaced by the pastor's own confession of how proud he was to be serving a beautiful church like this one, the way he showed his friends the expensive new windows and the fine fellowship hall. Then he confessed his realization that this was only part of the church, that there was much more to be said for mission and outreach.

Telling Our Story

One reason why Christians are Christians is that we have learned to listen to a certain story that is told in God's word. The scriptures provide us with the story of how God relates to us. The preacher is the one who puts the congregation in dialogue with that story. The Bible doesn't present us with a unified philosophical system. It presents us with a narrative, as complex and multifaceted as any narrative, of God's dealings with humanity. In each generation the church has laid alongside this master story our own stories and read the two together. The stories of Israel and the stories of Jesus provide the context whereby we are able to make sense out of our own stories today.

In the examples of sermons in this book, we have observed contemporary preachers attempting to speak to congregational problems by listening to our master biblical story and then telling that story alongside the congregation's story. Good stories rarely have simple endings. They are complex, often open-ended. They thereby draw us into the narrative, encouraging each of us to enter the story and finish it in our own way.

Long before psychotherapy with its insights into the phenomenon of resistance, Christian communicators struggled with how to say the truth so that people heard the truth. We preachers need to focus as much upon *how* the Bible preaches as upon *what* the Bible preaches. New Testament critic Dan O. Via has noted that the Bible tends to be "propositionless." Preachers who see sermons as mainly a matter of three propositions and a poem are at a serious disadvantage when preaching biblically, because such is not the typical biblical way of dealing with truth. The Bible deals with truth through a wide array of literary devices, each carefully selected in order to do something to the hearer. A parable of Jesus, for instance, isn't simply an archaic, homiletically primitive narrative vessel containing a valuable truth—the parable is an integral part of the truth. By the parable, Jesus is doing something to us that could not be done without the parable. Note that I did not say that the parable was telling us something or teaching us something—although it does. I said that it was doing something to us.

Sallie McFague notes that much biblical material, including parables, is "thick." That is, we are not simply to take a parable, dig beneath the surface, and mine the abstract truth contained in it. Rather, we are to attend to the nature of the parable itself, what it is doing to us by its characters, movement, and style. If, for instance, we preachers take the parable of the prodigal son, put it in an exegetical saucepan and boil it down to some abstract principle, we have not really dealt with the truth or our hearers as Jesus dealt with the truth and his hearers.

With the assistance of literary critics of scripture I am becoming more attentive to the literary quality of scripture, asking myself questions such as, "What is this particular type of biblical literature attempting to do to its audience?" In other words, I am asking, *"How* does this passage preach?" before I ask, *"What* does this passage preach?"

We are talking about style here, the mood of a text which is a valuable component in our hearing of the text. In preaching classes in seminary, we were usually taught to conceive of sermons as discourses about ideas. Style, color, and mood were thoroughly secondary sermon traits. The main thing was to get our ideas right. But the Bible frequently goes after truth in a much more dynamic way. A parable, for instance, does not simply want us to understand some new idea. Rather, it wants to throw us off balance, catch us off our guard, dislocate our world so that we might be relocated elsewhere.

Matthew's parable of the laborers in the vineyard catches us by surprise. In a gospel noted for its emphasis on rewards and punishments, just deserts, and accountability, the story of the latecomers who are paid the same wage as the persons who have sweated in the vines all day comes like a punch in the stomach. "What kind of way is this to run a world?" we ask. A little, predictable everyday story has ended unpredictably. The hearers are left, not with the smug realization that they have mastered a new concept about God, but with the shocked surprise that God's grace has thrown them off balance. If the audience reaction is, "Yes, that's the way we always imagined it, God is predictably gracious and accepting," then we may have preached the right idea, the "what" of the text, but we have failed to preach the text as Jesus preached it.

A distinguished preacher expounded upon the parable of the talents in our seminary chapel one morning. His sermon was a rather predictable, warmed-over power of positive thinking treatment: You and I have great talents that we must use to their fullest. He gave many examples of great people who have discovered hidden talents, acres of diamonds, and have gone on to become healthy, wealthy, and wise because they used their talents.

The next day a young seminarian preached on the same text. She simply read it and declared, "Here is a text about judgment. We shall all be judged. One day, all of us shall stand before God and render account." She spoke of her own fear of that moment of reckoning because, "You and I have been given so much. We are the beneficiaries of our country's best educational advantages. We have never known poor health care or malnutrition. We are the privileged, the elite. But one day, you and I shall be called to account. We shall hold our lives in the palms of our hands and be called upon to account for how we have used all this in the service of the Master." I think she got the text. The first sermon led to the smug, self-satisfying assurance that we are in control of our destiny, that we are like God in our ability to manipulate, control, and produce. No judgment there. The second sermon conveyed some of the bite that the original parable must have had. The medium is the message.

So a crucial exegetical question, particularly when we are attempting to let the scripture speak to some church conflict, is, "How does this text work at congregational conflict?"

We beat people over the head with our moralizing about should, ought, and must. The Bible tells them a story, and we respond to a dispirited congregation through a shrill call to do better and to be better. Paul sings them a hymn on the greatness of God, reminds them of the miracle of their choice in baptism, and speaks of them as royalty. Dealing with the truth in the way in which the Bible itself deals with the truth can lead to a better hearing by our listeners and a more faithful message for them to hear.

When They Say No

But none of this implies that if we just find the right words, exercise true empathy, and develop the best homiletical skills, our message on a particular congrega-

tional problem will be positively received. Right at the beginning of his Gospel, Luke takes Jesus to his hometown
synagogue in Nazareth—among the people who knew and
loved him, the people who most wished him success—and
shows us why Jesus failed. Jesus was sent to the cross, not
because he was an inept, nonempathetic preacher, but because he preached so well that it hurt. If he experienced
rejection, those of us who struggle to be faithful to his
words should not expect universal acceptance of our words.

Congregational resistance to the truth is powerful, not
because people are perverse (which, classical Christian
theology says, we all are), but because they are fearful,
holding on for dear life and doing about the best they can
with what they have. Patience is an essential pastoral virtue, a virtue that I do not have by natural inclination. Pastors must respect and love their people enough to allow
them to say no.

When Tom arrived as the new pastor at Shady Grove
Church, it did not take him long to realize that the bishop
was absolutely right when he told him, "Your major task will
be to get those folks at Shady Grove to realize that their
church must be relocated." Shady Grove had been built on
the edge of town in what was supposed to be a new area of
suburban growth. Unfortunately the new homes were built
elsewhere, and Shady Grove Church found itself in the unenviable position of being in an isolated corner of a busy
expressway that went through many acres of warehouses,
factories, railroad tracks, and other industrial ugliness.

But it didn't take Tom long to realize why his predeces-
sors at Shady Grove had been unsuccessful in their attempts
to relocate the congregation. The congregation now con-
sisted of people in their early fifties. They had already invested much time, love, and money in Shady Grove Church
and had no intention of pulling up stakes, admitting that
their chosen site was a mistake, and moving on.

Tom was still hopeful. In his sermons he tried to encourage the congregation to be open to "new possibilities," to
"dream bold dreams" and "reach out to new life." Without
mentioning the relocation issue, he hoped to prepare the
people for consideration of relocation.

"You don't fool us," said one of the longtime members.

"We know that the bishop sent you here to move us and that you will not rest until you do."

Tom continued to be patient, to visit the people, to work with them and love them. He decided to be more open with people, to admit that, after a year of work in the congregation, he was convinced that relocation was the best path for Shady Grove. On the Third Sunday after Pentecost he had the opportunity to speak directly to the issue. The first lesson was Solomon's prayer at the dedication of the Temple in Jerusalem: "Behold, heaven and the highest heaven cannot contain thee; how much less this house which I have built!" (1 Kings 8:27). Tom preached about the greatness of God and our inability to contain or limit God even in our most beloved buildings, even here at beloved Shady Grove.

As far as Tom's people were concerned, his opening sermonic volley was the last straw. Soon after his sermon, there was open rebellion. The pastoral relations committee petitioned the bishop to move Tom and send them another pastor, "who won't try to move us," and Tom was moved to another parish.

It would be good if I could report that Tom's patience, Tom's skill in preaching, Tom's pastoral sensitivity had changed the people at Shady Grove. Unfortunately that's not the way the story ended. The people who said no continued to say no. Tom was left with his grief that things did not change and with the need to pick up the pieces and begin ministry elsewhere.

That's the way it sometimes works when there is conflict in the church and problems in the pulpit.

We come into the ministry with certain lofty visions of the way the real church is supposed to look, the way real Christians are supposed to appear after really good preaching has had its way with them. But when we attempt to embody our vision in some particular parish, we find that no people can fully embody that vision. Jesus wept over Jerusalem because he realized that his vision of "the things that make for peace" would not be embodied fully in these people.

There is much of that sort of weeping, or at least silent groaning, in the pastoral ministry from time to time. If a preacher doesn't at least groan now and then over the gap between expectations and realization, then that preacher must have either lost the vision completely or else has become adept at denial of the facts of life in the church.

To locate our vision of the church in a particular place and people, St. John's on the Expressway, is to lodge it in a church that will dislodge it, sooner or later. For no person, no people, can ever become that responsible, that committed, that faithful. Yet good preaching demands that we invest ourselves with intensity, that we really preach to these people as if the fate of the kingdom of God rested on what is said and heard here today.

When what we hope is not heard, we feel grief. Pastors can swallow the grief, repudiate the vision, deny the investment they made in the task, and flee the ministry. We can flee by resigning and seeking other work or by degenerating into the cool and collected "professional," going about ministry, managing a church, refereeing in conflict like some religious robot.

Or the minister may cling to the vision, fully believing that the right word, the good sermon, the skillful approach, will solve everything—deny the limits of preaching, the limits of hearing, one's limits as a pastor, and pretend that the people are not saying no. Seek out the few in the congregation who seem to agree with you or find several ministerial tasks that seem to evoke response and invest in them to the neglect of preaching. Like the minister who has swallowed the grief and made peace with the pain, these ministers have also avoided the reality of the people's no.

The Bible says that, time and again, even when we said no, God said yes. What is scripture, if not the long story of all the ways that God has taken the initiative to restore a broken relationship, or at least maintained the patience to endure us when we were most unlovable? Time and again, in the silence after our rejection, this resourceful God has come out to love us and embrace us, to speak to us and begin again the eternal conversation.

The preacher reflects that divine resourcefulness, that godly patience, when he or she, even after having the words of the sermon rejected, misunderstood, or unheard last week, climbs up into the pulpit once again to speak. In so doing, the preacher reassures us, just by his or her presence, that God will not let us go, even when we say no, even when our lives cannot live up to the vision God has set before us. Fortunately, our community, the life of our congregation, is not dependent on our faithfulness, our ability to say yes. It is dependent upon God's willingness to take us back, to speak yes in the face of and in spite of our no.

That hope is the preacher's salvation, and in that hope, the preacher speaks, confident that the grace of God is sufficient.

Notes

1. Speed Leas and Paul Kittlaus, *Church Fights: Managing Conflict*, pp. 29–32.
2. Ibid., pp. 32–34.
3. Ibid., p. 48.
4. Larry L. McSwain and William C. Treadwell, Jr., *Conflict Ministry in the Church* (Nashville: Broadman Press, 1981), pp. 31, 49.
5. Ibid., pp. 44–45.
6. Alan C. Filley, *Interpersonal Conflict Resolution* (Glenview, Ill.: Scott, Foresman & Co., 1975), p. 25.
7. William H. Willimon, *Worship as Pastoral Care*, ch. 9.
8. Walter Brueggemann, *The Prophetic Imagination* (Philadelphia; Fortress Press, 1978), p. 13.
9. From "Embarrassed by the Church: Congregations and the Seminary," Stanley Hauerwas and William H. Willimon, *The Christian Century*, February 5–12, 1986, pp. 117–120, with additions.
10. Fred B. Craddock, *Preaching* (Nashville: Abingdon Press, 1985), p. 64.
11. Thomas Sieg, "Models of Preaching," *Worship*, vol. 59, no. 3 (May 1985), pp. 220–230.
12. Donald W. Shriver, Jr., ed., *The Unsilent South: Prophetic Preaching in Racial Crisis* (Atlanta: John Knox Press, 1965), p. 146.
13. Ibid., pp. 146–151.
14. Cited in Paul A. Mickey, Gary Gamble, and Paula Gilbert, *Pastoral Assertiveness: A New Model for Pastoral Care* (Nashville: Abingdon Press, 1978), pp. 103–104.
15. Craddock, *Preaching*, pp. 146–147.
16. Roger Fallot, "When Congregations Won't Listen," *The Christian Ministry*, March 1985, p. 15.
17. Ibid.

Bibliography

Glasse, James D. *Putting It Together in the Parish.* Nashville: Abingdon Press, 1972.

Leas, Speed, and Paul Kittlaus. *Church Fights: Managing Conflict in the Local Church.* Philadelphia: Westminster Press, 1973.

Mickey, Paul A., and Robert L. Wilson. *Conflict and Resolution: A Case-Study Approach to Handling Parish Situations.* Nashville: Abingdon Press, 1973.

Willimon, William H. *Integrative Preaching: The Pulpit at the Center.* Nashville: Abingdon Press, 1981.

———. *Preaching and Leading Worship.* Philadelphia: Westminster Press, 1984.

———. *Worship as Pastoral Care.* Nashville: Abingdon Press, 1979.